DR. COLBERT'S
HEALTHY
GUT ZONE
COOK
BOOK

DON COLBERT, MD

Published in the United States by Noble Way Media

First Edition

ISBN (Hardcover): 978-1-7378290-8-9

Printed in the United States of America

This book contains the opinions and ideas of its author. It is solely for informational and educational purposes and should not be regarded as a substitute for professional medical treatment. The nature of your body's health condition is complex and unique. Therefore, you should consult a health professional before you begin any new exercise, nutrition, or supplementation program or if you have questions about your health. Neither the author nor the publisher shall be liable or responsible for any loss or damage allegedly arising from any information or suggestion in this book.

The statements in this book about consumable products or food have not been evaluated by the Food and Drug Administration. The recipes in this book are to be followed exactly as written. The publisher is not responsible for your specific health or allergy needs that may require medical supervision. The publisher is not responsible for any adverse reactions to the consumption of food or products that have been suggested in this book.

CONTENTS

RECIPES

INTRODUCTION

What if I told you your gut is likely responsible for both disease and healing? The gut is the foundation of full-body health: it holds the key to healthy weight loss; a life with less brain fog, anxiety, and depression; a strong immune system; and an end to so many symptoms that make life less than vibrant.

From our very first breath, the gut plays a vital role in every single aspect of our lives. Be it our brains, metabolism, immunity, skin, or feelings—the gut impacts it all. Thankfully, our overall health is not based solely on the circumstances of our birth or even those first few months of life. How we started out matters a great deal, but how we eat and live from today forward is much more important. Your gut plays a primary role in your current and future health. Treat it well, make it healthy, and you will reap the many benefits.

I can't tell you how many patients have come to me suffering from swelling, bloating, gas, reflux, and similar bowel problems, who were then surprised to learn that many of their other health concerns were connected to their guts. A healthy gut will not only take care of your gut-related symptoms but will also often lessen and even eradicate a host of other ailments and diseases!

Many of today's medical experts are becoming aware of the vital importance of gut health, but few provide a health plan or lifestyle changes that give the gut—and the body—what it needs to be healthy and happy, both inside and out.

This cookbook is your ticket to that Healthy Gut Zone lifestyle. Did I mention it's also delicious? Inside, you'll find 100 recipes that avoid foods that commonly irritate the gut and instead put gut-healing ingredients front and center on your plate.

The gut is far more powerful than we ever knew. It has the power to change your health and your life completely, one meal at a time.

THE TRUTH ABOUT YOUR GUT

Your gut is your gastrointestinal tract (GI tract) and runs top to bottom, starting at your mouth, then extending through the esophagus, stomach, small intestine, and large intestine (colon) before ending at your rectum and anus—the last parts of your large intestine.

The purpose of the gut has always been viewed as the digestion of food and absorption of nutrients, vitamins, minerals, simple sugars, fatty acids, and amino acids. What went in was either used or discarded. And there was nothing more to report. It has been assumed for generations that our gut is pretty much indestructible. But that is not the case. Our gut is far less impervious or ironclad than we used to believe.

There are two main reasons for this:

1. **The gut is designed both to be permeable and to act as a barrier.** Absorbing nutrients, simple sugars, amino acids, fatty acids, vitamins, and minerals from the digested food into the bloodstream through the intestinal wall is part of the gut's job. It also acts as a barrier, preventing undigested food, proteins, fats, and toxins from being absorbed.

2. **The gut can spring leaks.** An increasing number of pro-

teins, foods, medicines, and bacteria have been found to, figuratively speaking, punch microscopic holes in the gut wall by damaging the tight junctions between the intestinal cells, allowing undigested food and toxins to leak through. For us to simply live, our gut must provide us with nutrients from the food we eat. If excessive breaches (microscopic holes) occur in the gut, it becomes more permeable. We develop a leaky gut (also called increased intestinal permeability), and our health is compromised.

It's not only organs and tissues that make up your gut; microbes also call the gut home. An excellent place to get a glimpse of the gut's importance is at the microscopic level. Amazingly, your gut holds one hundred trillion microbes (bacteria), and each one has its own DNA. These account for 90 percent of the total number of cells in your body! Yes, that means only 10 percent of your cells are human.

Most of these microbes are either harmless or beneficial for you. They provide an invaluable service, which includes breaking down indigestible food, supplying your gut with energy, making vitamins, breaking down toxins and medications, and training your immune system to defend itself. The trillions of microbes living in your gut comprise what is called **a microbiome**.

If you collected that microbiome into a single jar, it would weigh up to five pounds and would consist primarily of these four phyla of bacteria: Actinobacteria, Proteobacteria, Firmicutes, and Bacteroidetes. The latter two make up more than 90 percent of our gut microbes.

We all have these microorganisms living in our gut (especially in the large intestine or colon) in differing amounts. Only recently have we found that the ratio or balance of microbes in the gut directly influences your health. It makes sense, then, that your gut and your microbiome need to be healthy for you to be healthy.

I have treated countless patients who displayed many of these same symptoms. Every symptom is usually a telltale sign of a leaky gut. When we healed their leaky guts, they usually found the relief, fix, or cure they needed.

SYMPTOMS OF A LEAKY GUT

Aching joints · Acid reflux or heartburn · Acne · Age spots · Allergies · Alopecia · Anemia · Arthritis · Asthma · Autoimmune diseases (thyroid disease, rheumatoid arthritis, type 1 diabetes, multiple sclerosis, Crohn's, colitis, lupus) · Bone loss (osteopenia and osteoporosis) · Brain fog · Cancer · Canker sores · Chronic fatigue syndrome · Chronic pain syndrome · Colon polyps · Cramps, tingling, numbness · Decline in dental health · Dementia · Depression · Diabetes, prediabetes, insulin resistance · Dizziness · Ear ringing · Exhaustion · Fibromyalgia · Gastroesophageal reflux disease (GERD) · Gastrointestinal problems (bloating, pain, gas, constipation, diarrhea) · Headaches · Heart disease · Hypertension · IBS · Infertility · Irregular menstrual cycle · Irritability · Low testosterone · Low white blood cell count · Lymphomas · Malabsorption like low iron · Male-pattern baldness · Memory loss · Migraine headaches · Parkinson's disease · Peripheral neuropathy · Skin rashes · Skin tags · Vitiligo · Weight gain · Weight loss

---

There are two basic steps to fixing a leaky gut:

1. **Step 1: Get rid of the bad.** Remove offending foods, bad or excessive bacteria and yeast, parasites, medications, toxins, and more. Learn to cope with stress.
2. **Step 2: Eat more of the good.** Recharge the gut with good bacteria in the form of probiotics and sometimes prebiotics, and regularly eat foods that support the gut.

That's it in a nutshell. When you remove the things that trigger a leaky gut and then recharge the gut with healthy foods, your gut has the power to heal. I have seen severe health situations start to turn around in as little as two weeks after removing the bad and replacing it with quality, gut-healthy foods. More often, it takes four to six weeks for an undeniable change to take place, and within three months, the symptoms are usually gone or greatly reduced.

The bottom line? Keeping your gut healthy is one of the best things you can do for your overall and long-term health.

THE SEVEN CAUSES OF LEAKY GUT

Before we can talk about health, losing weight, or giving your body the food it needs, we must first stop the gut from leaking. Leaky gut is due to chronic inflammation. But what causes that inflammation in the first place? For decades we have medicated rather than fixed the real issues in our bodies, but now we know that when the gut stops leaking, the body is usually able to heal itself.

Here are the prevailing causes of leaky gut, from most common to least common:

1. ANTIBIOTICS

The most common cause of a leaky gut is the overuse of antibiotics—whether from the prescriptions we take or the food we eat. Antibiotics are designed to kill off bad bacteria that are causing sickness or infection, and they have saved countless lives doing just that. The problem is that with each dose, the good bacteria are put through the same regimen and they die along with the bad bacteria. A single course of antibiotics is enough to mess up your good gut bacteria for an entire year!

The secondary problem is that we overuse antibiotics, viewing them as miracle cures to treat anything and everything that afflicts us. This over-zealous use puts our gut health—and our overall health—at risk.

Thirdly, the livestock and poultry industry use 80 percent of the antibiotics sold in the US. For decades, antibiotics have been used to fatten farm animals. When we eat those antibiotic-fed animals, the same fattening process may be happening to us.

2. NSAIDS

The second biggest cause of a leaky gut is something that will probably surprise most people. Have you taken any of these?

- aspirin
- celecoxib (Celebrex)
- ibuprofen (Motrin, Advil)
- meloxicam (Mobic)
- naproxen (Aleve, Naprosyn)
- another nonsteroidal anti-inflammatory drug (NSAID)

Though they may bring temporary relief to pain, in return, these nonsteroidal anti-inflammatory drugs damage the gut wall, increasing gut permeability. This can lead to even greater damage to your body than the pain relief was worth.

3. ACID-BLOCKING MEDS

Acid-blocking drugs are a significant cause in leaky gut. Whether prescribed or purchased without a prescription, acid blockers treat heartburn, acid reflux, GERD, and other acid-related symptoms, such as ulcer disease, gastritis, and more. The immediate goal is to reduce stomach acid. However, your body needs stomach acid to function properly. The primary purpose of stomach acid is to digest the food you eat. Eliminate that acid and your body is less efficient in its work of digestion.

The following acid blockers are commonly used:

- Dexilant
- Nexium
- Prevacid
- Prilosec
- Protonix
- Zegerid

Blocking stomach acid provides temporary relief from heartburn or reflux. However, stomach acid kills bacteria, and lack of stomach acid enables bacteria to flourish—especially bad bacteria. This imbalance is bad news for your gut! Your body desperately needs stomach acid, so don't get rid of it. If you are told you need antacids, find an alternative that addresses the real issues, not one that masks one symptom but then brings with it a host of other problems. See my book *Healthy Gut Zone: Heal Your Digestive System to Restore Your Body and Renew Your Mind* for natural, gut-friendly alternatives.

4. GMO FOODS

Much can and needs to be said about genetically modified organism (GMO) foods. It is naïve to think that pesticides, insecticides, or herbicides that destroy pests and diseases on a plant will pass through the human body without doing any damage. GMO foods were not introduced to the US food supply until the 1990s. Approved by the FDA but banned in many other countries, GMO foods include these well-known food crops:

- alfalfa
- canola (for oil)
- corn

- cotton (used to make cottonseed oil)
- papaya
- soy
- sugar beets (used to make granulated sugar)

As the food cycle continues, GMO foods (especially corn) are fed to animals. That includes the beef, poultry, and fish industries, and this trickles right back to us in the meat, milk, cheese, eggs, and farm-raised fish we eat. Gastrointestinal disorders have been on the rise for the past fifty years, which means GMOs are not the only cause. But GMO foods do play a big role in the gut issues we face today.

Since GMO foods seem to be everywhere, what can we do? Thankfully we live in a day and age where we have a lot of other options. First, eat organic as much as possible. Look for a certified organic seal or a non-GMO statement on the food and produce you buy. Second, don't eat the most common GMO foods, such as corn and soy, unless they are clearly marked as non-GMO.

It will take a little time to adjust your food buying habits, so be patient with yourself. Go slowly. You don't have to double your food budget or go hungry. Begin the process by avoiding GMO foods. It won't be long before you settle into a rhythm of finding the right food choices for your lifestyle and budget.

5. CHLORINE IN DRINKING WATER

Chlorine has been added to water for more than one hundred years. It has done wonders to prevent cholera and typhoid the world over, but like antibiotics, it also kills off good bacteria. While chlorine in water does not pose the same level of toxicity to your gut as antibiotics, it still negatively impacts the beneficial bacteria in your GI tract.

Despite all the benefits that chlorine has brought to countries around the world, we need to do the best we can to minimize our absorption of chlorine. You get it into your system when you drink it, go swimming, or take a shower. It's even in the steam in the bathroom during a hot shower. Here are a few ways to avoid drinking or cooking with chlorine laden tap water:

- If you have a chlorine swimming pool, consider converting it to a saltwater pool
- Consider installing a water filtration system on your entire house
- Drink bottled water
- Invest in a water filter for your kitchen that removes chlorine
- It might seem silly, but if you shorten your shower time and keep the water slightly cooler so there is no steam to inhale, you can reduce your chlorine exposure considerably (or purchase and install a shower filter)

You may not be able to avoid it altogether, but the less chlorine in and on your body, the better.

6. PESTICIDES

Over one thousand different pesticides are used around the world, each with unique properties and effects on their intended source. The most common way pesticides enter your body is from what you eat and drink, but these pesticides are also found in such places as bug sprays, lawn care products, and even the air during mosquito-spraying season. Pesticides do damage by killing some of your good gut bacteria, allowing the bad bacteria to overpopulate.

Even if pesticides cause minimal damage to your gut bacteria, repeated exposure, even in small doses, can eventually add up. In this case, every exposure is eliminating good bacteria. And you need all the good bacteria you can get.

Minimize your interaction with pesticides by watching what you eat, reading ingredients in the bug sprays and lawn care products you use, and washing fruits and vegetables before eating.

7. INTESTINAL INFECTIONS

Although this final cause of a leaky gut is one of the top seven, it is not all that common. What puts intestinal infections on the list is the fact that, many times, they lead to IBS and leaky gut. Intestinal infections can be serious; they often have a long-term negative impact and can even be deadly. The best way to treat intestinal infections is also the best way to live life, and that is with high levels of good bacteria in your gut.

As you can see, the most common causes of a leaky gut are such a large part of modern life that it's no wonder so many of us are suffering from a whole host of gut-related symptoms. Now that you know what has been secretly damaging your gut, it's time to protect yourself from further damage and get the relief and healing your body deserves.

TEN COMMON ENEMIES OF YOUR GUT

Aside from resolving leaky gut, your long-term health journey requires an understanding of the offending foods, toxins, and behaviors that attribute to gut issues. Once you remove the bad from your life, it is much easier to replace your gut enemies with healthy foods and lifestyle choices. If you have an unhealthy gut, these are usually the ten most common enemies your gut is fighting:

1. GLUTEN

The most common enemy to your gut is gluten. Gluten is the protein found in wheat, barley, and rye, as well as all the bread, pasta, bagels, pretzels, cereals, cakes, cookies, and processed foods made with these gluten-rich flours. If your gut is not healthy, I would recommend that you go gluten-free for at least six months to a full year. After your gut has healed itself, you may consider re-introducing small and occasional amounts of gluten. Until then, you should avoid gluten altogether.

2. A HIGH-SUGAR, HIGH-CARB DIET

The second-greatest cause of inflammation and increased leaky gut that I see is a high-sugar, high-carb diet. Bacteria usually grow unchecked in a sugary environment. Naturally, it is not good bacteria that thrive in the gut when we consume high-sugar and high-carb foods. We can (and should) eat foods that help to control inflammation and keep our *good* bacteria levels high. That means not eating what everyone else is eating. High-sugar, high-carb diets will not help anyone live a healthy life.

3. DAIRY

It is no surprise that dairy is on the list of the most common enemies of your gut. It regularly ranks as one of the top items to which people are allergic or sensitive. In fact, cow's milk is the number one food allergen around the world. The sugar in milk (lactose) causes digestive problems known as lactose intolerance and can also contribute to gut inflammation. For those who are working to restore their gut to healthy levels, I strongly recommend going dairy free for a minimum of several months. This provides enough time for good gut bacteria to replenish and gut inflammation to decrease.

4. LECTINS

According to some, lectins are likely found in around 30 to 40 percent of the foods we typically eat in the American diet. They are primarily concentrated in grains (especially wheat), seeds, nuts, legumes (especially soy), nightshade plants (potatoes, tomatoes, eggplant, peppers, etc.), and dairy. Lectins are proteins that plants use as a self-defense mechanism against predators. If you feel bad after you have eaten something, it could very well be your body reacting to the lectins. Weight gain, bloating, gas, and brain fog are often lectins working against you.

5. ARTIFICIAL SWEETENERS

The next common enemy to your gut, gut wall, and overall health is artificial sweeteners. These fake sugars, or "noncaloric artificial sweeteners" (NAS), have been recognized as bad for your health for years. Just how bad and what they do to your body are becoming more evident as time goes by.

Here are common artificial sweeteners to avoid:

- acesulfame potassium (brand names: Sunett, Sweet One, Sweet & Safe)
- alitame (brand name: Aclame)
- aspartame (brand names: NutraSweet, Equal, Spoonful, Equal-Measure, Canderel, Benevia, AminoSweet, NatraTaste)
- aspartame-acesulfame salt (brand name: Twinsweet)
- cyclamate (brand names: Sucaryl, Cologran)
- saccharin (brand names: Sweet'N Low, Necta Sweet, Cologran, Heremesetas, Sucaryl, Sucron, Sugar Twin, Sweet 10)
- sucralose (brand names: Splenda, Nevella)

6. EMULSIFIERS

The best way to describe an emulsifier is to think of it as a chemical that allows you to mix two different liquids, like oil and water. Oil and water naturally separate from each other, but with an emulsifier added, the two ingredients can be mixed and stay mixed. Emulsifiers offer many more options for the prepared food industry in terms of ingredients, consistency, smoothness, shelf life, and visual appeal. As you can imagine, these "detergent-like molecules" do real damage to your gut, gut wall, and good bacteria.

7. SATURATED FATS

Most saturated fat in our diets comes from meats or animal products, but plants also contain saturated fat. Saturated fat causes the release of lipo-polysaccharide (LPS), an endotoxin that is bad for your gut and gut wall.

The primary sources of saturated fats include:

- Beef
- Butter
- Cheese
- Cocoa Butter
- Coconut Milk
- Coconut Oil
- Cream
- Ice Cream
- Pork
- Sour Cream
- Palm Oil

A simple test is to look at fats at room temperature. If fats are in a solid state at room temperature, then they are saturated fats and should be avoided or minimized. If they are liquid, such as avocado oil or olive oil, then they are unsaturated fats or monounsaturated fats and are better for consumption.

8. CONSTIPATION

Your gut needs to be able to process foods in about twenty-four to forty-eight hours. Good gut motility is a necessary part of your good health. In other words, constipation should not be a regular part of your daily routine. If it is, you need to do what it takes to restore your gut health.

9. STRESS

Stress slows down digestion, helping the bad bacteria and harming the good. It also reduces the body's ability to properly absorb nutrients and minerals from the foods you eat. I have seen stress mess with people's metabolisms, causing them to gain weight. When you subdue the stressors in your life, your gut health automatically improves. Conversely, the stronger and healthier your gut is, the better you can handle stress.

10. STAYING TOO CLEAN

The last common enemy of the gut may seem a little outrageous, but it makes sense when you see the facts. Many of us are too clean. Cleanliness is said to be next to godliness, but it seems we have gotten a bit carried away with our efforts to eradicate bacteria in our homes, on our hands, and in the air. Being clean and reducing bacteria are fine but trying to live in a sterile world (home, body, office) without dirt or bacteria takes things too far.

GUT HEALING FOODS SHOPPING LIST

Now that you are aware of the gut enemies in your life, it's time to fill your home and kitchen with foods that aid your gut in healing. Put these foods at the top of your shopping list while on the Healthy Gut Zone diet.

Veggies: artichokes, arugula, asparagus, basil, beets, bok choy, broccoli, brussels sprouts, cabbage (Chinese, green, red), carrots, cauliflower, celery, chives, cilantro, cucumbers (if peeled and deseeded), garlic, greens (collard, dandelion, field, mustard), kale, kimchi, kohlrabi, lettuce (butter, romaine, green leaf, red leaf), mint, mushrooms, okra, olives, onions (all types), parsley, perilla, purslane, radishes, sauerkraut, scallions, seaweed, spinach, Swiss chard, tomatoes (if peeled and deseeded), watercress

Dairy: Avoid all dairy for one to three months. After that, use cheese (goat, sheep, feta), grass-fed butter, grass-fed ghee, goat milk kefir, goat milk yogurt, milk (goat or A2 milk rather than A1)

Meat: beef, bison, elk, lamb, moose, venison (all known to be or listed as grass-fed and grass-finished); chicken, duck, eggs, goose, pheasant, quail, turkey (all known to be or listed as organic and free-range, not fed soybeans); anchovies, bass, calamari, clams, crab, halibut, lobster, mussels, oysters, salmon, sardines, scallops, shrimp, tongol tuna (all known to be or listed as wild)

Nuts and seeds: almonds, Brazil nuts, chestnuts, coconut, flaxseeds, hazelnuts, macadamia, pecans, pine nuts, pistachio, psyllium, walnuts (Note that peanuts and cashews are not nuts but legumes.)

Beverages: coffee; tea (black, green); filtered water, spring water, or sparkling water with lemon or lime wedge

Chocolate: low sugar, dark (72 percent or higher)

Fats: avocado, MCT, nut, and olive oils

Fermented foods: kimchi, pickles, sauerkraut

Flours: almond, arrowroot, cassava, coconut, green banana, plantain, sweet potato flour

Fruits: avocado and berries—blueberries, blackberries, raspberries, strawberries (These are the best due to their low sugar content.)

Resistant starches: green banana, green mango, green papaya, jicama, parsnips, rutabaga, sweet potato, taro root, yams, yucca

Seasonings: anise, basil, capers, celery seed, cinnamon, cloves, cocoa powder, cumin, curry powder, ginger, oregano, peppermint, rosemary, saffron, sage, spearmint, thyme

Starches: flax bread, millet bread, sweet potatoes, yams, cassava, carrots, taro root, yucca, jicama, tortillas (from cassava, cassava and coconut, or almond by Siete brand), and bread made from almond, coconut, or cassava, such as Julian Bakery paleo bread (Add Indian basmati white rice after avoiding for at least one month.)

Supplements: prebiotics, probiotics, psyllium husk powder, and, if needed, vitamin D3, hydrolyzed collagen, L-glutamine, magnesium, omega-3 (See appendix D.)

Sweeteners: erythritol, Just Like Sugar (inulin), monk fruit sugar, stevia

BREAKFAST

Many popular breakfast foods—like pancakes, cereal with milk, muffins, and fruit juices—work against a healthy gut, but that doesn't mean you can't enjoy your favorite morning meals. With a little creativity, almost all breakfast flavors can be recreated with gut-friendly ingredients. Along with a Gut Zone breakfast, I like to start my morning with a cup of organic coffee with MCT oil and a bit of dark cocoa powder. The coffee and cocoa are rich in polyphenols, and the MCT oil is a safe and healthy saturated fat and does not raise LPS levels like coconut oil. This gut-friendly "mocha" keeps me satisfied and ready to take on the day.

VEGETABLE FRITTATA

A perfect way to make use of the vegetable odds and ends in your fridge, this Italian-inspired spin on the classic omelet is finished in a hot oven and makes a beautiful centerpiece for a weekend or holiday meal. Though this recipe uses mushrooms and greens, feel free to substitute any gut-healing vegetables, like broccoli, asparagus, or artichokes to make it your own.

PREP
20 MIN

COOK
25 MIN

SERVES
6

INGREDIENTS

- 8 large eggs, organic free-range
- 2 tablespoons fresh flat-leaf parsley, finely chopped
- ¾ teaspoon kosher salt, divided
- ½ teaspoon freshly ground black pepper
- ¼ cup extra virgin olive oil
- ½ cup yellow onion, peeled and chopped
- 1 cup button mushrooms, washed and sliced
- 1 clove garlic, peeled and minced
- 1 cup baby spinach, washed and dried
- 1 cup baby arugula, washed and dried

DIRECTIONS

Preheat the oven to 400°F with the oven rack in the middle. In a medium bowl, whisk together eggs, parsley, ½ teaspoon salt and ½ teaspoon pepper.

In a large (12") cast iron or non-stick, oven-safe skillet, heat olive oil over medium heat. Add the onions and ¼ teaspoon salt, and cook, stirring occasionally, until they are translucent, about 5 to 7 minutes.

Add the mushrooms and cook, stirring occasionally, until heated through and just beginning to brown, about 4 to 6 minutes. Stir in the garlic and cook until just fragrant, about 1 minute.

Turn the heat off the stove and add the egg mixture, spinach, and arugula to the vegetables in the skillet. Use tongs to distribute the vegetables evenly among the egg mixture. Transfer the skillet to the oven and bake until the eggs are set, and the top is lightly golden around the edges, 15 to 20 minutes. Let cool slightly before slicing into wedges and serving.

NUTRITION FACTS
Amount per serving | Calories 185 | Total Fat 16.1g | Saturated Fat 3.4g | Cholesterol 248mg | Sodium 136mg | Total Carbohydrate 2.4g | Dietary Fiber 0.6g | Total Sugars 1.2g | Protein 9.1g

BAKED EGGS WITH SPINACH AND SALMON

PREP
25 MIN

COOK
25 MIN

SERVES
4

Delicate salmon has long enjoyed a place on the breakfast table—think bagels and lox and Swedish open-faced sandwiches topped with dill-flecked fish. In this recipe, salmon gets a Gut Zone makeover in elegant individual baked egg dishes fit for company. As always, low-mercury wild Alaskan salmon is the best choice. For a more filling start to your day, add a boost of healthy fat and fiber with some avocado slices.

INGREDIENTS

- ¼ cup extra virgin olive oil, plus more for greasing
- 5 cups baby spinach, washed
- ¾ pound salmon fillet, boneless, skinless, cut into 1-inch pieces
- 1 teaspoon salt, divided, plus more for water
- 1 teaspoon freshly ground black pepper, divided
- 4 large eggs, organic free-range
- 2 tablespoons chives, snipped

DIRECTIONS

Preheat the oven to 350°F. Lightly grease four ovenproof ramekins with olive oil and arrange in a small roasting dish or a cake pan. Have a large bowl of ice water ready.

Bring a large pot of heavily salted water to a boil over high heat. Add the spinach and cook until wilted, 1 to 2 minutes. Drain well and submerge the spinach in the bowl of iced water to stop the cooking. Drain again and wring dry using a cloth kitchen towel.

Divide the spinach and salmon evenly between the ramekins. Divide ½ teaspoon each salt and pepper evenly among the 4 ramekins. Create pockets in each ramekin and crack an egg into them. Drizzle each with 1 tablespoon olive oil and season them all with the remaining ½ teaspoon salt and ½ teaspoon pepper.

Carefully fill the pan with enough hot water so that it comes about halfway up the sides of the ramekins. Bake until eggs are set and the salmon is cooked through and opaque in appearance, 15 to 20 minutes.

Carefully remove the roasting pan from the oven. Use tongs to transfer the ramekins to serving plates. Sprinkle chives on top of the eggs and serve immediately.

NUTRITION FACTS
Amount per serving | Calories 377 | Total Fat 29g | Saturated Fat 5.6g | Cholesterol 250mg | Sodium 745mg | Total Carbohydrate 2.2g | Dietary Fiber 1g | Total Sugars 0.6g | Protein 28.5g

FRESH HERB OMELET WITH GREEN PEAS AND ONIONS

Fresh herbs are rich in antioxidants and can take a simple omelet into gourmet territory with virtually no effort. They're also incredibly easy to grow at home in a patio container or even a sunny windowsill. When you grow your own herbs, you can simply snip off as much as you need and avoid extras wilting in the produce drawer.

PREP
5 MIN

COOK
10 MIN

SERVES
1

INGREDIENTS

- 3 large eggs, organic free-range
- 1 tablespoon fresh parsley
- 1 tablespoon fresh dill
- 1 teaspoon fresh thyme
- ¼ teaspoon kosher salt
- ¼ teaspoon freshly ground black pepper
- 1 teaspoon avocado oil
- ½ sweet onion, peeled and sliced
- 1 clove garlic, minced
- ¼ cup green peas (fresh or frozen, thawed)

DIRECTIONS

In a small bowl, beat together eggs, parsley, dill, and thyme. Season with salt and pepper. Set aside.

Heat oil in a nonstick pan over medium heat. Add onion and garlic. Sauté until tender, 3 to 5 minutes. Increase heat to medium-high and add the green peas.

Pour egg mixture into the pan. Eggs should start to set immediately at the edges. Gently move the mixture around the pan, so all portions cook evenly. Fold the omelet in half and slide the omelet onto a plate. Serve immediately.

NUTRITION FACTS
Amount per serving | Calories 323 | Total Fat 19.9g | Saturated Fat 5.3g | Cholesterol 558mg | Sodium 805mg | Total Carbohydrate 15.5g | Dietary Fiber 4.2g | Total Sugars 5.6g | Protein 22.5g

SAUTÉED WILD MUSHROOMS WITH POACHED EGGS

PREP
10 MIN

COOK
20 MIN

SERVES
4

In addition to offering a delicious and exciting change from the everyday button mushroom, wild mushrooms deliver a wide range of health benefits. They're a good source of B vitamins, Vitamin D, and anti-inflammatory and cognitive-boosting compounds. Pro tip: to keep your mushrooms fresh as long as possible, avoid washing them until just before you're ready to use them.

INGREDIENTS

- 6 tablespoons extra virgin olive oil
- 1 pound fresh wild mushrooms, cleaned and sliced, i.e., oyster, shiitake, cremini, etc.
- 4 cloves garlic, peeled and minced
- ½ teaspoon salt, or more to taste
- ½ teaspoon freshly ground black pepper, or more to taste
- 3 tablespoons fresh chives, thinly sliced, plus more for garnish
- 2 teaspoons red wine vinegar
- 4 large eggs, organic free-range

DIRECTIONS

In a large cast iron or non-stick skillet, heat olive oil over medium-high heat. Add the mushrooms and cook, flipping occasionally, until browned, 5 to 8 minutes.

Add garlic, salt, and pepper and stir until the garlic is fragrant, about 1 minute. Turn off the heat and stir in the chives. Set aside.

Meanwhile, in a large high-sided skillet, bring 6 cups of water to a boil over high heat, then lower the heat to barely a simmer. Add vinegar to the water.

Crack an egg into a small bowl and gently slip the bowl into the water, releasing the egg. Use a rubber spatula to gently push the egg white closer to the yolk to better hold it together. Repeat this process with the remaining three eggs, adding all the eggs to the same pan while leaving some distance between them. Simmer, uncovered, until the whites are opaque, and the yolks are still runny, 3 to 6 minutes.

Divide mushrooms between 4 plates. Use a slotted spoon to place an egg on top of each of the 4 plates of mushrooms. Season to taste with more salt and pepper, if desired, and garnish with chives. Serve immediately.

NUTRITION FACTS
Amount per serving | Calories 222 | Total Fat 19.3g | Saturated Fat 3.6g | Cholesterol 186mg | Sodium 368mg | Total Carbohydrate 5.4g | Dietary Fiber 1.3g | Total Sugars 2.4g | Protein 10.1g

SWEET POTATO "TOAST" WITH AVOCADO AND SMOKED SALMON

While gluten-laden toast may be off the menu while you work on healing your gut, you can still enjoy your favorite toast toppings with this handheld breakfast of sliced, baked sweet potatoes. Avocado and smoked salmon offer a great, gut-friendly hit of healthy fats and protein, but the toast options are truly endless—from almond butter and berries to fresh salsa and a fried egg. You can even make a big batch of baked sweet potato slices and store them in the freezer for a quick reheat in the toaster.

PREP
15 MIN

COOK
45 MIN

SERVES
4

INGREDIENTS

- 2 medium sweet potatoes, scrubbed
- 3 tablespoons extra virgin olive oil
- 1 teaspoon salt
- 1 teaspoon freshly ground black pepper
- 1 avocado, pitted, peeled, and thinly sliced
- ¾ pound smoked salmon, wild caught (12 oz.)
- 2 tablespoons fresh flat-leaf parsley, finely chopped

DIRECTIONS

Preheat oven to 425°F. Line a baking sheet with parchment paper, set aside.

Slice the sweet potatoes crosswise into ½-inch-thick rounds and place them on the prepared baking sheet. Drizzle the sweet potatoes with olive oil and sprinkle with salt and pepper. Roast the sweet potatoes, flipping halfway through cooking, until they are brown and crispy on the edges, 40 to 45 minutes.

Remove the sweet potato rounds from the oven and divide them evenly among 4 plates. Top each round with equal amounts of avocado and smoked salmon and sprinkle with chopped parsley. Serve immediately.

NUTRITION FACTS
Amount per serving | Calories 374 | Total Fat 21g | Saturated Fat 3.3g | Cholesterol 20mg | Sodium 2296mg | Total Carbohydrate 30.3g | Dietary Fiber 7g | Total Sugars 0.6g | Protein 18g

GRAIN-FREE GRANOLA

PREP
15 MIN

COOK
15 MIN

SERVES
4

Most conventional granola is full of sugar and grains that won't keep you full (or keep your gut happy). Instead, try this nut-powered granola for a snack or breakfast atop some unsweetened coconut yogurt or a baked sweet potato. Because they are so rich in healthy unsaturated fats, nuts are prone to spoilage at room temperature. To extend the shelf life of your almonds, pecans, hazelnuts, walnuts, and other nuts, store them in the fridge or freezer.

INGREDIENTS

- ½ cup raw whole almonds, coarsely chopped
- ½ cup raw pecan halves, coarsely chopped
- ¼ cup raw hazelnuts, coarsely chopped
- ¼ cup raw macadamia nuts, coarsely chopped
- ¼ cup extra virgin olive oil
- ½ cup blanched almond flour
- 1 ¼ cups unsweetened shredded coconut
- ⅓ cup monk fruit sugar
- 2 teaspoons ground cinnamon
- ½ teaspoon salt

DIRECTIONS

Preheat oven to 350°F. Line a standard-sized baking sheet with parchment paper. Set aside.

In a large mixing bowl, add the almonds, pecans, hazelnuts, macadamia nuts, olive oil, almond flour, shredded coconut, monk fruit sugar, cinnamon, and salt. Mix well until combined and then spread out on the prepared baking sheet.

Bake the granola, stirring halfway through cooking, until golden brown in parts, 7 to 15 minutes. Allow the granola to cool to room temperature before eating. Store the granola at room temperature in an air-tight container for up to 3 weeks.

NUTRITION FACTS

Amount per serving | Calories 553 | Total Fat 53.4g | Saturated Fat 21g | Cholesterol 0mg | Sodium 302mg | Total Carbohydrate 14.6g | Dietary Fiber 8g | Total Sugars 3.1g | Protein 7.1g

GREEN MANGO AND COCONUT SMOOTHIE

Green mango is an excellent source of resistant starch, the fiber that resists digestion in your small intestine and slowly ferments in your large intestine. There, it can feed the good bacteria that help your gut thrive. Green mango is also an exceptionally rich source of vitamin C! (If you like your smoothies a little sweeter, add some stevia or monk fruit sugar to taste.)

PREP
5 MIN

COOK
5 MIN

SERVES
2

INGREDIENTS

- 2 cups unsweetened almond milk, vanilla flavor
- 1 large green mango, peeled, pitted, and cut into chunks
- ½ cup unsweetened shredded coconut
- 8 large ice cubes

DIRECTIONS

Add all ingredients to a blender pitcher and blend on high until smooth. Pour into 2 glasses and enjoy immediately.

NUTRITION FACTS
Amount per serving | Calories 210 | Total Fat 10.8g | Saturated Fat 6.4g | Cholesterol 0mg | Sodium 186mg | Total Carbohydrate 29.8g | Dietary Fiber 5.4g | Total Sugars 23.8g | Protein 3g

AVOCADO AND SPINACH SMOOTHIE

PREP
5 MIN

COOK
5 MIN

SERVES
2

Avocado is one of my favorite healthy, whole food fats. It's a nutritious source of monounsaturated fats, fiber, magnesium, and potassium, and it can be added to savory or sweet foods—this smoothie is a great example! For an extra creamy smoothie, try freezing your avocados when they are about to get too ripe. Some grocery stores also sell affordable, pre-frozen bags of avocados.

INGREDIENTS

- 1 ½ cups baby spinach, washed and dried
- ½ medium avocado, peeled, pitted, and diced
- 2 cups low fat coconut milk
- ½ teaspoon stevia
- Ice cubes

DIRECTIONS

Place all the ingredients except for the ice in a blender. Blend on high for 20 seconds or until smooth. Fill two glasses with ice and add the smoothie. Serve immediately.

NUTRITION FACTS
Amount per serving | Calories 205 | Total Fat 19.2g | Saturated Fat 7.7g | Cholesterol 0mg | Sodium 22mg | Total Carbohydrate 8.3g | Dietary Fiber 5.4g | Total Sugars 1.2g | Protein 2.5g

SAVORY VEGGIE CHILLER

Most juices are fruit (and sugar) bombs, but fresh vegetable juice can be a delicious way to enjoy a flavorful and nutrient-packed refresher in the morning. This zesty, colorful blend of beets, carrots, and savory spices is unlike anything you'll find at a typical juice bar!

PREP
5 MIN

COOK
5 MIN

SERVES
2

INGREDIENTS

- 1 cup fresh beetroot juice, either freshly pressed or purchased
- 1 cup fresh carrot juice, either freshly pressed or purchased
- ½ cup kefir
- 2 teaspoons fresh lemon juice
- ¼ teaspoon ground cumin
- ¼ teaspoon salt
- ¼ teaspoon freshly ground black pepper
- Ice cubes
- fresh parsley leaves, for garnish (if desired)

DIRECTIONS

Add juices, kefir, and lemon juice to a blender pitcher, along with the cumin, and blend. Season with salt and pepper. Add ice cubes to 2 glasses, fill with the vegetable drink, and serve garnished with parsley. Enjoy immediately.

NUTRITION FACTS

Amount per serving | Calories 191 | Total Fat 2.5g | Saturated Fat 1.4g | Cholesterol 8mg | Sodium 440mg | Total Carbohydrate 38.1g | Dietary Fiber 2.8g | Total Sugars 23.4g | Protein 5.9g

BAKED EGGS IN AVOCADO

PREP
5 MIN

COOK
15 MIN

SERVES
4

This breakfast combines two of nature's nearly perfect foods: avocado and eggs. Together, they provide a filling meal with plenty of gut-friendly fats, fiber, and protein to keep you fueled—you can even bake them ahead of time for a compact snack that tastes as good cold as it does right out of the oven. Avoid using extra-large eggs for this dish, as smaller eggs will better fit inside the avocado and avoid spillover.

INGREDIENTS

— 2 medium avocados

— 4 large eggs, organic free-range

— 1 teaspoon dried oregano

— ¼ teaspoon kosher salt, or more to taste

— ¼ teaspoon freshly ground black pepper, or more to taste

DIRECTIONS

Preheat oven to 400°F.

Halve the avocados and remove pit. Scoop out a little flesh to create pockets for the eggs.

Arrange the avocado halves on a rimmed baking sheet and carefully crack eggs into each of them. Sprinkle with oregano, salt, and pepper.

Bake until the eggs set, 12 to 15 minutes. Remove from the oven and serve immediately.

NUTRITION FACTS
Amount per serving | Calories 217 | Total Fat 18.3g | Saturated Fat 3.4g | Cholesterol 186mg | Sodium 224mg | Total Carbohydrate 8.2g | Dietary Fiber 6.1g | Total Sugars 0.7g | Protein 8g

BREAKFAST TACOS ON CASSAVA TORTILLAS

If you've ever been to Austin, Texas, you'll no doubt have fallen in love with breakfast tacos—a great option for breakfast, lunch, or dinner! I love serving these for company as everyone can customize their tacos to their liking. Cassava tortillas are gluten-free and have plenty of resistant starch, making them a gut-friendly alternative to flour and corn tortillas. Top your tacos with avocado slices for an extra filling meal.

PREP
10 MIN

COOK
25 MIN

SERVES
4

INGREDIENTS

- 4 tablespoons extra virgin olive oil, divided
- 2 cups cremini mushrooms, washed and sliced
- 1 ½ teaspoons salt, divided
- 1 teaspoon freshly ground black pepper, divided
- 8 large eggs, organic free-range
- 3 cups baby spinach leaves, washed and dried, thinly sliced
- 8 cassava tortillas (approx. 7 oz. package)

DIRECTIONS

Preheat the oven to 175°F. Place the tortillas on a standard-sized baking pan. (It is okay if they overlap.) Place in the oven to warm while preparing the rest of the ingredients.

In a medium skillet, heat 2 tablespoons olive oil over medium-high heat. Add the mushrooms and cook, flipping a few times during cooking until browned, 6 to 8 minutes. Season the mushrooms with ¾ teaspoon salt and ½ teaspoon pepper. Set aside.

In a medium bowl, whisk the eggs with the remaining ¾ teaspoon salt and ½ teaspoon pepper.

In a large cast iron or non-stick skillet, heat the remaining 2 tablespoons olive oil over medium heat. Add the eggs and cook, stirring occasionally until just cooked through and scrambled, about 3 to 6 minutes. Set aside.

Remove the tortillas from the oven and place two tortillas on each of 4 plates. Evenly divide the mushrooms, eggs, and spinach over the tortillas and fold each tortilla in half over the toppings. Serve immediately.

NUTRITION FACTS
Amount per serving | Calories 384 | Total Fat 25.5g | Saturated Fat 5.4g | Cholesterol 372mg | Sodium 1054mg | Total Carbohydrate 24.8g | Dietary Fiber 3.9g | Total Sugars 1.9g | Protein 16.9g

13

TOASTED COCONUT FLOUR WAFFLES WITH COCONUT SPRINKLES

PREP
20 MIN

COOK
15 MIN

SERVES
4

Waffles definitely belong in a healthy gut lifestyle, they just require some savvy swapping and topping to avoid gluten and excess sugar. This recipe is made with coconut flour, which is extremely absorbent—that's why you only need a ½ cup for the full recipe. Be sure to let the batter rest for 10 minutes before making your waffles, as this allows the flour to fully absorb the liquid ingredients and reach the proper consistency.

INGREDIENTS

- ½ cup unsweetened shredded coconut, divided
- 2 teaspoons vanilla extract, divided
- 4 large eggs, organic free-range
- ½ teaspoon monk fruit sweetener
- ¼ teaspoon salt
- 2 tablespoons avocado oil
- 6 tablespoons light coconut milk
- ½ cup coconut flour
- ¼ teaspoon baking powder
- avocado oil cooking spray

DIRECTIONS

In a small sauté pan, toast the shredded coconut with 1 teaspoon of vanilla extract over medium heat, stirring occasionally until golden brown. Set aside.

Preheat waffle iron according to the manufacturer's instructions.

In a large mixing bowl, combine ¼ cup prepared toasted coconut, eggs, monk fruit sweetener, salt, avocado oil, coconut milk, and remaining 1 teaspoon of vanilla extract. Whisk just until smooth.

Add the coconut flour and baking powder and beat until no longer lumpy. Let stand for 10 minutes.

Spray the waffle iron with cooking spray. Spoon the batter into the iron and close. Cook for 2 to 3 minutes or until golden. Remove waffle from the iron and keep warm. Cook the remaining batter.

Serve waffles sprinkled with remaining toasted coconut.

NUTRITION FACTS
Amount per serving | Calories 377 | Total Fat 23.2g | Saturated Fat 15.7g | Cholesterol 186mg | Sodium 313mg | Total Carbohydrate 27.7g | Dietary Fiber 16.4g | Total Sugars 5.2g | Protein 13.2g

MILLET AND SWEET POTATO BREAKFAST PARFAITS

This warm, comforting breakfast is a good substitute for oatmeal in the morning—especially on a cool fall day when adding pumpkin spice to everything just feels right. Millet is one of the only grains (along with sorghum) that contain no lectins, and sweet potato offers resistant starch to support your gut healing journey.

PREP
20 MIN

COOK
10 MIN

SERVES
4

INGREDIENTS

- ½ cup unsweetened almond milk
- 2 teaspoons orange zest
- 1 can sweet potato purée, (15 oz.)
- ½ teaspoon white miso paste
- ½ teaspoon pumpkin pie spice
- 1 teaspoon vanilla extract
- ½ teaspoon stevia, divided, plus more to taste
- ½ cup millet, prepared
- ¾ cup unsweetened coconut yogurt
- ¼ cup walnuts, toasted
- ¼ cup unsweetened coconut flakes, toasted, plus more for garnish

DIRECTIONS

In a medium saucepan over medium heat, combine milk and orange zest and warm through without boiling, about 2 to 3 minutes.

Add the sweet potato, white miso paste, pumpkin pie spice, vanilla, and half of the stevia. Combine until the mixture has thickened. Remove from heat and set aside.

Add a pinch of stevia to the cooked millet and stir.

Layer and alternate the ingredients in four large glasses, starting with the millet, followed by yogurt, walnuts, and sweet potato mixture. Repeat. Top with reserved coconut flakes. Serve immediately. Top with reserved coconut flakes for serving.

NUTRITION FACTS
Amount per serving | Calories 263 | Total Fat 14.2g | Saturated Fat 8g | Cholesterol 0mg | Sodium 74mg | Total Carbohydrate 29.8g | Dietary Fiber 6.5g | Total Sugars 1.8g | Protein 4.8g

CASSAVA CREPES WITH COCONUT YOGURT
AND MINT-CILANTRO CHUTNEY

PREP
10 MIN

COOK
35 MIN

SERVES
6

A sophisticated and savory spin on pancakes, these cassava crepes, featuring polyphenol-rich curry powder, are great for any meal. You can fill these crepes with greens, mushrooms, or protein like chicken or steak for a flavorful gluten-free wrap.

INGREDIENTS

MINT-CILANTRO CHUTNEY
- ¾ cup unsweetened coconut yogurt, divided
- ⅓ cup fresh mint leaves, finely chopped
- ¼ cup fresh cilantro leaves, finely chopped
- 1 small shallot, peeled and diced
- ¼ teaspoon stevia
- 1 lime, juiced
- ¼ teaspoon salt, or more to taste

CREPES
- 3 large eggs
- 4 tablespoons avocado oil, plus more for frying
- ½ teaspoon white miso paste
- ¼ teaspoon curry powder
- ¼ teaspoon salt
- ¾ cup cassava flour
- 2 cups unsweetened almond milk

DIRECTIONS

For the mint-cilantro chutney, combine ¼ cup coconut yogurt with the remaining ingredients in a medium bowl. Set aside.

Combine all the ingredients for the crepes in a large bowl and mix until a smooth batter forms.

Heat a mid sized non-stick skillet with two teaspoons of additional avocado oil over medium-high heat. Cooking one crepe at a time, spread ¼ cup of the crepe batter throughout the bottom of the pan. Cook for a few minutes until golden and then flip for another 30 seconds to 1 minute before removing the crepe from the pan. Repeat until the batter is gone. Grease the pan with additional oil as needed while making the remaining crepes.

Serve the crepes warm alongside the mint-cilantro chutney and remaining yogurt for dipping, spreading, or stuffing the crepes.

NUTRITION FACTS
Amount per serving | Calories 235 | Total Fat 16.6g | Saturated Fat 3.5g | Cholesterol 94mg | Sodium 473mg | Total Carbohydrate 18.9g | Dietary Fiber 2.8g | Total Sugars 0.5g | Protein 4g

SPICED SWEET POTATO BREAKFAST BOWLS

This comforting bowl is like enjoying a slice of warm pumpkin pie for breakfast! Gut-friendly MCT oil is a safe and healthy saturated fat that will not raise LPS levels. The combination of fiber and good fats in the bowl's toppings buffer the carb content of the sweet potatoes, keeping your blood sugar stable through the morning.

PREP
10 MIN

COOK
60 MIN

REST
20 MIN

SERVES
4

INGREDIENTS

— 2 medium sweet potatoes, scrubbed

— 1 cup unsweetened almond milk

— ¾ teaspoon ground cinnamon

— ½ teaspoon ground ginger

— ⅛ teaspoon ground cloves

— 2 tablespoons MCT oil

— 1 teaspoon salt

— ½ cup raw pecans, coarsely chopped

— ½ cup unsweetened coconut flakes

— 2 teaspoons flax seeds

DIRECTIONS

Preheat oven to 400°F.

Use the tines of a fork to poke holes all over the sweet potatoes. Wrap each sweet potato in aluminum foil and place on a baking sheet. Bake the sweet potatoes until fork tender, 45 minutes to 1 hour. Let the sweet potatoes cool slightly, about 20 minutes, before peeling and transferring to a large bowl.

Use a potato ricer or masher and mash the sweet potatoes until smooth. Stir in almond milk, cinnamon, ginger, and cloves until well combined.

Divide the sweet potato mixture between 4 bowls. Top each bowl of sweet potato with 2 teaspoons MCT oil, ¼ teaspoon salt, 2 tablespoons pecans, 2 tablespoons coconut flakes, and ½ teaspoon flax seeds. Serve warm or at room temperature.

NUTRITION FACTS
Amount per serving | Calories 265 | Total Fat 13.4g | Saturated Fat 9.3g | Cholesterol 0mg | Sodium 630mg | Total Carbohydrate 33.3g | Dietary Fiber 6.3g | Total Sugars 1g | Protein 2.9g

17

VEGETABLE AND EGG BREAKFAST BOWLS WITH MILLET

PREP
20 MIN

COOK
5 MIN

SERVES
2

This colorful, nutrient-packed vegetarian bowl is big on flavor and gut-friendly ingredients like kimchi, jicama, avocado, and prebiotic-rich wakame seaweed. Double the recipe and compose bento-style bowls for lunch on the go! (Simply toss the avocado with a bit more lime juice to prevent browning.)

INGREDIENTS

- ⅓ cup jicama, peeled and finely chopped
- 2 teaspoons lime juice
- ¼ teaspoon kosher salt, or more to taste
- 2 cups mixed leaf lettuce, washed and torn
- ½ cup millet, prepared according to package directions
- 1 tablespoon dried wakame seaweed, bloomed in water and drained according to package directions
- 1 large avocado, peeled, pitted, and sliced
- ¼ cup kimchi
- 1 tablespoon extra virgin olive oil
- 2 large eggs
- 2 green onions, thinly sliced
- 2 tablespoons toasted pumpkin seeds
- 1 teaspoon toasted sesame oil
- ½ teaspoon freshly ground black pepper, or more to taste
- ½ teaspoon kosher salt, or more to taste

DIRECTIONS

In a small bowl, toss the chopped jicama together with lime juice and salt.

In two bowls, add equal amounts of lettuce, millet, wakame, avocado, kimchi, and dressed jicama. Set aside.

Heat olive oil in a large non-stick frying pan over medium heat. Crack the eggs into the pan. Fry until the whites and yolks are set, 4 to 5 minutes. Remove eggs from pan and add to salad bowls.

Top each salad bowl with a sprinkling of green onion, pumpkin seeds, and drizzled sesame oil. Add freshly ground pepper and kosher salt to taste.

NUTRITION FACTS

Amount per serving | Calories 354 | Total Fat 24g | Saturated Fat 4.9g | Cholesterol 186mg | Sodium 1017mg | Total Carbohydrate 26.2g | Dietary Fiber 7.7g | Total Sugars 4.3g | Protein 12.8g

GREEN SHAKSHUKA WITH SPINACH AND PINE NUTS

Shakshuka is a classic North African dish of eggs poached in a flavorful spiced pepper and tomato sauce. This spin on the dish substitutes the tomatoes (which, as nightshades, can trigger inflammation) for spiced spinach and leeks. Feel free to pump up the green goodness and phytonutrients even more with fresh herbs like parsley and cilantro.

PREP
20 MIN

COOK
15 MIN

SERVES
4

INGREDIENTS

- 4 tablespoons extra virgin olive oil, divided
- 1 large leek, light green parts only, washed, halved lengthwise, and sliced thin
- 1 clove garlic, peeled and finely chopped
- 1 teaspoon ground coriander
- 1 teaspoon salt, divided
- 1 teaspoon freshly ground black pepper, divided
- 12 cups baby spinach, washed and dried (approx. 12 oz.)
- 8 large eggs, organic free-range
- ⅓ cup raw pine nuts

DIRECTIONS

Preheat oven to 400°F.

In a large 12-inch oven-proof skillet, heat 2 tablespoons olive oil over medium heat. Add the leek, garlic, coriander, ½ teaspoon salt, and ½ teaspoon pepper and cook, stirring occasionally, until the leek has softened, 6 to 8 minutes.

Add spinach to the pan by the handful, cooking until each handful has wilted before adding the next one, about 4 minutes total. Turn off heat.

Use a large spoon to create 8 pockets in the vegetables in the skillet and crack an egg into each one. Season the eggs with the remaining ½ teaspoon salt and ½ teaspoon pepper. Transfer the skillet to the oven and bake until the eggs are set and the yolks are slightly runny, 10 to 15 minutes.

Meanwhile, heat the remaining 2 tablespoons olive oil in a small skillet set over medium heat. Add the pine nuts and cook, stirring constantly, until golden, about 1 to 3 minutes.

Remove the shakshuka skillet from the oven and sprinkle with the pine nuts. Serve immediately.

NUTRITION FACTS

Amount per serving | Calories 376 | Total Fat 32.1g | Saturated Fat 5.7g | Cholesterol 372mg | Sodium 798mg | Total Carbohydrate 9.3g | Dietary Fiber 3g | Total Sugars 2.4g | Protein 17.1g

SWEET POTATO HASH

PREP
10 MIN

COOK
45 MIN

SERVES
6

Reminiscent of classic homestyle diner food, this simple sweet potato hash is a nutrient-dense stand-in for potato home fries or hash browns. Pair with a few fried eggs and some herbed chicken breakfast sausage (see p. 21) for a gut-friendly breakfast fit for even the heartiest appetites.

INGREDIENTS

- 4 tablespoons extra virgin olive oil, divided
- 2 large red onions, peeled and sliced
- ½ teaspoon kosher salt, or more to taste
- 3 large sweet potatoes, scrubbed and cut into bite-size pieces
- 4 cloves garlic, peeled and minced
- ½ teaspoon freshly ground black pepper, or more to taste
- 1 bunch fresh chives, finely chopped

DIRECTIONS

Preheat oven to 450ºF. Line a baking sheet with aluminum foil or parchment paper.

Add 1 tablespoon of olive oil to a large skillet set over medium-high heat. Once hot, add onions and season with salt. Reduce heat to medium and sauté the onions, frequently stirring, for 15 to 20 minutes, or until softened and caramelized.

Meanwhile, place the sweet potatoes in a large bowl, add minced garlic and remaining 3 tablespoons of olive oil, season with pepper, and toss to coat. Set aside.

Add sautéed onions to the bowl of sweet potatoes and combine. Spread the sweet potato mixture in a single layer on the prepared baking sheet—roast for 30 to 35 minutes, or until the sweet potatoes are fork-tender and crispy.

Transfer the hash to a serving platter. Garnish with fresh chives and serve hot.

NUTRITION FACTS

Amount per serving | Calories 252 | Total Fat 9.6g | Saturated Fat 1.4g | Cholesterol 0mg | Sodium 54mg | Total Carbohydrate 40.4g | Dietary Fiber 6.3g | Total Sugars 2.8g | Protein 2.7g

HERBED CHICKEN BREAKFAST SAUSAGES

Not all savory breakfasts need to include eggs. These homemade chicken sausage patties will ensure you get enough protein to fuel your day, while offering a welcome change from egg-centric dishes. Thyme, rosemary, and sage put an herbaceous spin on the classic breakfast sausage flavor, but you can feel free to experiment with other additions, like smoked paprika or fennel seeds to create your ideal house blend.

PREP
10 MIN

COOK
20 MIN

SERVES
4

INGREDIENTS

— 2 teaspoons fresh thyme leaves, finely chopped

— 1 teaspoon fresh rosemary, finely chopped

— 1 clove garlic, peeled and minced

— 1 ½ teaspoons ground sage

— 1 teaspoon salt

— 1 teaspoon freshly ground black pepper

— 1 pound ground chicken, organic free-range

— 3 tablespoons extra virgin olive oil, plus more if desired

DIRECTIONS

In a large bowl, combine the thyme, rosemary, garlic, sage, salt, and pepper. Add the chicken and use your hands or a large wooden spoon to mix well. On a cutting board, form the mixture into 12 equally sized patties.

In a large cast iron or heavy bottomed skillet, heat the oil over medium heat. Add the sausage patties to the skillet and cook, flipping halfway through cooking, until browned on both sides and cooked through, 10 to 12 minutes total. Repeat the process using more oil until all sausage patties are cooked. Transfer to a plate to rest for about 5 minutes before serving.

NUTRITION FACTS

Amount per serving | Calories 256 | Total Fat 19.7g | Saturated Fat 4.1g | Cholesterol 96mg | Sodium 649mg | Total Carbohydrate 1.3g | Dietary Fiber 0.6g | Total Sugars 0g | Protein 19.7g

SAVORY CAULIFLOWER BREAKFAST MUFFINS

PREP
15 MIN

COOK
45 MIN

SERVES
4

If you only think of muffins as sweet, prepare to be amazed by these savory delights. Perfect for a breakfast on the go, these cauliflower muffins could even be used as the base of a gut-friendly breakfast sandwich. Simply slice one in half and stuff with scrambled egg and an herbed chicken breakfast sausage patty (see p. 21)!

INGREDIENTS

- 1 medium cauliflower, finely chopped (approx. 2 ½ cups)
- ⅔ cup coconut flour
- 2 teaspoons salt
- 1 teaspoon freshly ground black pepper
- ½ teaspoon baking powder
- ¼ cup fresh chives, thinly sliced
- 2 tablespoons shallot, peeled and finely chopped
- 1 tablespoon fresh thyme leaves, finely chopped
- 7 large eggs, organic free-range
- ⅓ cup extra virgin olive oil

DIRECTIONS

Preheat the oven to 400°F. Line 8 cups of a standard-sized muffin pan with cupcake liners.

In a large bowl, stir together the cauliflower, coconut flour, salt, pepper, baking powder, chives, shallot, and thyme leaves.

In a separate medium bowl, whisk together the eggs and olive oil. Add the wet ingredients to the dry ingredients and stir until a smooth batter forms.

Use an ice cream scoop or large spoon to evenly divide the batter into the prepared cupcake liners. Transfer the muffin pan to the oven and bake until the muffins are golden brown on top and cooked through, 30 to 45 minutes. Remove from the oven and let rest 20 minutes before serving.

NUTRITION FACTS

Amount per serving | Calories 463 | Total Fat 30.7g | Saturated Fat 10.2g | Cholesterol 326mg | Sodium 1405mg | Total Carbohydrate 30.3g | Dietary Fiber 16.6g | Total Sugars 6.7g | Protein 19.2g

CARROT HASH BROWNS

Low in FODMAPS and rich in soluble fiber, polyphenols, and prebiotics, carrots are a worthy addition to any meal. I love to find new ways to use carrots beyond slicing them raw for salads and snack plates. Bright orange and slightly sweet, swapping potatoes for shredded carrots offers a fun way to shake up the breakfast routine.

PREP
15 MIN

COOK
20 MIN

SERVES
4

INGREDIENTS

- ¼ cup extra virgin olive oil
- 16 medium carrots, trimmed, scrubbed, peeled, and grated (approx. 8 cups)
- 1 ½ teaspoons salt
- 1 teaspoon freshly ground black pepper
- 1 teaspoon garlic powder
- ¼ cup fresh flat-leaf parsley, chopped

DIRECTIONS

In a large skillet, heat olive oil over medium-high heat. Add the carrots and cook, stirring occasionally until crisp tender, 8 to 10 minutes.

Add salt, pepper, and garlic powder to the carrots and stir to combine. Continue to cook the carrots until they are golden brown in parts and cooked through, 8 to 10 more minutes. Stir in the parsley and serve immediately.

NUTRITION FACTS
Amount per serving | Calories 213 | Total Fat 12.7g | Saturated Fat 1.8g | Cholesterol 0mg | Sodium 1043mg | Total Carbohydrate 25.1g | Dietary Fiber 6.3g | Total Sugars 12.2g | Protein 2.3g

CASSAVA PANCAKES

PREP
10 MIN

COOK
16 MIN

SERVES
4

Made from the root of the yuca plant, cassava flour acts and tastes much like wheat flour in baking. Due to the increasing popularity of gluten-free and nut-free baking, you can now find cassava flour at many supermarkets and online. I like using non-GMO verified, organic cassava flour from Otto's Naturals.

INGREDIENTS

— 1 ¼ cups cassava flour

— ⅓ cup coconut flour

— 2 teaspoons baking powder

— 2 tablespoons monk fruit sugar, plus more for serving

— ½ teaspoon salt

— 4 large eggs, organic free-range

— 1 ¼ cups unsweetened almond milk

— 6 tablespoons avocado oil, divided, plus more if necessary

— 1 lemon, cut into wedges, for serving

DIRECTIONS

In a large bowl, whisk together the cassava flour, coconut flour, baking powder, monk fruit sugar, and salt.

In a separate medium bowl, whisk together the eggs, almond milk, and 4 tablespoons oil. Add the wet ingredients to the dry ingredients in the large bowl. Use a large spoon to stir until combined. Let the batter rest for about 5 minutes.

In a large cast iron or non-stick skillet, heat the remaining oil over medium heat. Once hot, add the batter to the skillet in batches, using about ¼ cup batter for each pancake. Make sure to leave room between the pancakes in the skillet for easy flipping. Cook the pancakes until there are bubbles in the center and the bottom is lightly browned, 2 to 4 minutes per side. Transfer the pancakes to a serving plate and repeat the process with the remaining batter, adding more oil to the skillet if needed.

Serve the pancakes with a squeeze of fresh lemon juice from the lemon wedges and sprinkle with monk fruit sugar if desired.

NUTRITION FACTS

Amount per serving | Calories 270 | Total Fat 10.8g | Saturated Fat 3.7g | Cholesterol 186mg | Sodium 573mg | Total Carbohydrate 35.7g | Dietary Fiber 9.2g | Total Sugars 1.6g | Protein 9g

CHICKEN AND BRUSSELS SPROUT HASH

Brussels sprouts for breakfast? You bet. The key is slicing them thinly, as seen in this savory and filling one-pan breakfast. If you're not a fan of Brussels sprouts, feel free to swap in other cruciferous vegetables like broccoli, cauliflower, cabbage, kale, or radishes. (If you're feeling extra hungry, a fried egg and some avocado slices are delicious additions.)

PREP
15 MIN

COOK
20 MIN

SERVES
4

INGREDIENTS

- ¼ cup extra virgin olive oil
- 1 shallot, peeled and finely chopped
- 1 pound ground chicken, organic free-range
- 2 cloves garlic, peeled and minced
- 1 teaspoon fresh sage leaves, finely chopped
- 1 teaspoon fresh rosemary leaves, finely chopped
- 2 ¾ teaspoons salt
- 1 teaspoon freshly ground black pepper
- 1 pound Brussels sprouts, cleaned, ends trimmed, very thinly sliced (approx. 6 cups)
- ¼ cup fresh flat-leaf parsley, chopped

DIRECTIONS

In a large high-sided skillet, heat olive oil over medium-high heat. Add shallots and cook, stirring occasionally, until soft, 2 to 4 minutes.

Add chicken, garlic, sage, rosemary, salt, and pepper, and cook, breaking up the chicken and stirring occasionally, until the chicken is cooked through and browned in parts, 5 to 8 minutes.

Add the Brussels sprouts to the chicken and cook, tossing them occasionally, until they are tender but still bright green, 4 to 6 minutes. Stir in the parsley and serve immediately.

NUTRITION FACTS
Amount per serving | Calories 327 | Total Fat 22.2g | Saturated Fat 4.6g | Cholesterol 96mg | Sodium 1700mg | Total Carbohydrate 12.6g | Dietary Fiber 4.7g | Total Sugars 2.5g | Protein 23.8g

LUNCH

Here's a good rule of thumb for a gut-friendly lunch: aim to fill one-half to two-thirds of your plate with raw or cooked veggies. Vegetables form the foundation of the Healthy Gut Zone diet because they provide so much of what your gut needs the most. Personally, I enjoy a large salad with lots of veggies and a small amount of grilled chicken breast with grilled onions and a lot of high-phenolic extra virgin olive oil for lunch every day. Here, I share some of my other favorite salads, soups, and other vegetable-centric dishes inspired by the healthiest ingredients and vibrant flavors from cuisines around the world.

TUNA TARTARE IN ENDIVE BOATS

Treat yourself to a tapas-style lunch with a plate of delicate endive leaves filled with fresh tuna tartare. To easily chop the fish, try cutting it while slightly frozen—an hour in the freezer will make fresh tuna much easier to work with. (Hosting company? This dish also makes an elegant gut-friendly appetizer for a dinner party.)

PREP
10 MIN

COOK
10 MIN

SERVES
4

INGREDIENTS

- 2 large heads endive, yellow or red
- 1 pound tuna, sushi grade, finely chopped
- 1 avocado, pitted, peeled, and finely diced
- 2 tablespoons fresh cilantro, finely chopped
- 1 green onion, bulb removed, rinsed, and finely chopped
- 1 tablespoon extra virgin olive oil
- 1 tablespoon fresh lime juice
- ¼ teaspoon kosher salt, or more to taste

DIRECTIONS

Separate the leaves from each endive, wash, dry, and set aside.

In a medium bowl, combine tuna, avocado, cilantro, green onion, and olive oil. Season to taste with lime juice and salt; stir to combine.

Spoon the tuna tartare into each endive leaf. Serve immediately.

NUTRITION FACTS

Amount per serving | Calories 321 | Total Fat 12.7g | Saturated Fat 2.5g | Cholesterol 86mg | Sodium 116mg | Total Carbohydrate 4.7g | Dietary Fiber 3.7g | Total Sugars 0.4g | Protein 46g

CARROT BEET SALAD WITH WALNUTS

PREP
15 MIN

SERVES
4

This salad is a great way to enjoy nature's vibrant colors and sweetness without overwhelming your gut with too much sugar. Carrots are also rich in gut power tools like polyphenols and prebiotic fiber, so dig in! Be sure to pair it with some gut-friendly protein for a full meal.

INGREDIENTS

- 3 medium beets (red or yellow), peeled and grated
- 6 medium carrots, peeled and grated
- ½ cup raw walnut halves, coarsely chopped
- 1 cup flat-leaf parsley
- ¼ cup extra virgin olive oil
- 2 tablespoons fresh lemon juice
- 1 teaspoon salt
- ½ teaspoon freshly ground black pepper

DIRECTIONS

In a large bowl, combine beets, carrots, walnuts, and parsley.

In a small bowl, whisk together olive oil, lemon juice, salt, and pepper.

Pour the dressing over the carrot mixture and use tongs to toss until well combined. Serve the salad immediately or within a couple of hours.

NUTRITION FACTS
Amount per serving | Calories 320 | Total Fat 24.2g | Saturated Fat 3g | Cholesterol 0mg | Sodium 750mg | Total Carbohydrate 25.7g | Dietary Fiber 6.4g | Total Sugars 16.4g | Protein 5.7g

CAULIFLOWER CAKES WITH VEGAN MINT YOGURT SAUCE

Cauliflower is a great way to up your insoluble fiber intake, and this fresh and flavorful dish will make eating your fill a joy. Serve over greens for a fiber-filled lunch and your gut will thank you. Fun fact: it's the stems that have the most insoluble fiber, so be sure to grate those into your cauliflower cakes along with the florets.

PREP
5 MIN

COOK
30 MIN

SERVES
4

INGREDIENTS

MINT YOGURT

— ¾ cup coconut yogurt, unsweetened (vegan)

— 2 tablespoons mint, finely chopped

— 2 scallions, sliced (green tops only)

— ¼ teaspoon kosher salt, or more to taste

CAULIFLOWER CAKES

— 3 cups cauliflower florets and stems (approx. 1 pound)

— 2 large eggs, organic free-range

— 2 tablespoons coconut flour, plus extra for dusting

— 1 tablespoon ground flax meal

— 1 scallion, finely sliced

— ⅓ cup mint, leaves only, sliced, plus extra for serving

— ½ teaspoon kosher salt

— ¼ teaspoon freshly ground black pepper

— 4 tablespoons extra virgin olive oil, plus 1 tablespoon more for serving

DIRECTIONS

In a mixing bowl, combine the yogurt, mint, scallions, and kosher salt. Set aside.

Grate the cauliflower using a box grater or the grating attachment of a food processor. Place in a steaming basket, cover, and steam over a half-filled saucepan of simmering water until tender, 3 to 5 minutes. Transfer cauliflower to a large mixing bowl. Add eggs, coconut flour, flax meal, scallion, mint, and salt and pepper, beating until a consistent mixture forms. Add more coconut flour as needed. Divide and shape into eight small round cakes between damp hands. Dust with additional coconut flour, shaking off the excess.

Heat two tablespoons of olive oil in a large non-stick frying pan set over medium heat. Working in two batches, arrange four cakes in the pan, frying until golden-brown, 2 to 3 minutes per side.

Repeat the process for remaining cakes. Serve cauliflower cakes drizzled with mint yogurt dipping sauce and remaining olive oil.

NUTRITION FACTS

Amount per serving | Calories 293 | Total Fat 21.6g | Saturated Fat 4.8g | Cholesterol 93mg | Sodium 534mg | Total Carbohydrate 19.2g | Dietary Fiber 9.2g | Total Sugars 5.3g | Protein 8.9g

AVOCADO AND CARROT SALAD
WITH MISO-CARROT DRESSING

PREP
10 MIN

COOK
5 MIN

SERVES
4

Most store-bought salad dressings contain gut-busting dairy, sugar, and preservatives, but you don't need to settle for boring dressings to help your body feel its best. This savory-sweet dressing will become a fast favorite and looks beautiful drizzled over just about any salad or vegetable. Make a double batch to keep in the fridge for future meals!

INGREDIENTS

DRESSING

— 1 ½ teaspoons Dijon mustard

— 3 tablespoons carrot juice, preferably fresh or cold-pressed

— 2 teaspoons white miso paste

— 1 tablespoon white wine vinegar

— 6 tablespoons extra virgin olive oil

— ⅛ teaspoon kosher salt

— ⅛ teaspoon freshly ground black pepper

TO ASSEMBLE

— 6 cups arugula, washed and dried

— 1 cup of canned hearts of palm, sliced into discs

— 3 medium carrots, cleaned, peeled, and shredded (approx. 1 cup)

— 1 avocado, halved, pitted, peeled, and roughly sliced

DIRECTIONS

In a small mixing bowl, combine the mustard, carrot juice, miso paste, and vinegar. Whisk the oil in a slow, steady stream until the dressing is thickened and emulsified. Add salt and pepper, adding more to taste.

Scatter the arugula between serving plates. Top with hearts of palm, carrots, and avocado. Spoon over some of the dressing, serving the remainder on the side. Enjoy immediately.

NUTRITION FACTS

Amount per serving | Calories 294 | Total Fat 28.5 | Saturated Fat 4.6g | Cholesterol 0mg | Sodium 476mg | Total Carbohydrate 11g | Dietary Fiber 4.7g | Total Sugars 2.7g | Protein 2.4g

AVOCADO, LIME, AND COCONUT SOUP

PREP
10 MIN

SERVES
2

On a warm summer day, this zesty no-cook meal that's ready in minutes hits the spot. Full of healthy fats, it will also keep you satisfied longer than a typical tomato-packed gazpacho. Pair it with a fresh salad and leftover salmon for a full meal without heating the kitchen. Pro tip: use a high quality extra virgin olive oil to drizzle over the soup, and the flavor and color will really shine.

INGREDIENTS

— 1 medium avocado, halved, pitted, and peeled

— ½ cup low-fat coconut milk

— ¼ cup unsweetened, non-dairy yogurt

— ¼ cup white onion, peeled and chopped

— 1 lime, zested and juiced

— ¼ teaspoon kosher salt

— ½ tablespoon extra virgin olive oil, for plating

— 1 tablespoon cilantro, finely chopped

DIRECTIONS

Place all ingredients except olive oil and cilantro (to be reserved for plating) in a blender. Blend until smooth, and add additional salt and lime juice to taste, if desired. If the soup is too thick, you can loosen it with additional lime juice or cold water.

Place the soup in bowls and drizzle with extra virgin olive oil. Then, garnish with cilantro. This dish can be served chilled or served immediately at room temperature.

NUTRITION FACTS

Amount per serving | Calories 268 | Total Fat 21.3g | Saturated Fat 4.2g | Cholesterol 0mg | Sodium 303mg | Total Carbohydrate 20.8g | Dietary Fiber 9.8g | Total Sugars 7g | Protein 4.4g

GRILLED SARDINES (SARDE ALLA GRIGLIA)

PREP
20 MIN

COOK
10 MIN

SERVES
4

Sardines are among the healthiest (and most affordable) seafood options. Nutrient dense, full of gut-friendly unsaturated omega-3 fats, sustainably caught, and boasting the lowest levels of mercury of any fish, sardines are really a nutritional hero. While sardines are widely available smoked in tins, this recipe borrows a method from Sicily for grilling fresh sardines, served simply with some herbs and a splash of lemon.

INGREDIENTS

- 1 ½ pounds fresh sardines, cleaned and gutted, heads and tails intact
- 3 tablespoons extra virgin olive oil, plus extra for drizzling
- 1 clove garlic, peeled and finely chopped
- 1 teaspoon fresh thyme leaves, chopped
- ½ teaspoon salt
- ½ teaspoon freshly ground black pepper
- 1 lemon, cut into wedges, for serving

DIRECTIONS

Preheat grill or grill pan to medium heat. If using a grill, have a grill basket ready.

In a small bowl, whisk together olive oil, garlic, thyme, salt, and pepper.

Brush the sardines with the olive oil mixture. If using a grill, place the sardines into the grill basket. Grill until cooked through and just beginning to brown, 3 to 4 minutes per side.

Transfer the fish to a serving platter. Drizzle with more olive oil, sprinkle with more salt and pepper, if desired, and garnish with lemon wedges. Serve immediately.

NUTRITION FACTS
Amount per serving | Calories 213 | Total Fat 14.9g | Saturated Fat 2.7g | Cholesterol 0mg |
Sodium 521mg | Total Carbohydrate 2.5g | Dietary Fiber 0.8g | Total Sugars 0.5g | Protein 1.4g

GRILLED SHRIMP SKEWERS
WITH LIME AND HERBS

PREP
15 MIN

Shopping for shrimp can be a little confusing for the uninitiated. The number that you see next to the shrimp shows you how many shrimp are in a pound—the smaller the number, the larger the shrimp. Frozen shrimp are typically a better bet than "fresh" as they will have been frozen since they were caught. (The "fresh" shrimp at the seafood counter is most likely thawed shrimp that was previously frozen!) Wild caught shrimp will taste cleaner and fresher than farmed, and will be better for your gut, too.

COOK
10 MIN

SERVES
4

INGREDIENTS

- 8 10-inch skewers, metal or wood
- ¼ cup extra virgin olive oil
- 1 tablespoon fresh lime zest
- 2 cloves garlic, peeled and minced
- 1 tablespoon fresh chives, thinly sliced, plus more for garnish
- 1 teaspoon fresh dill sprigs, finely chopped, plus more for garnish
- 1 teaspoon fresh mint, finely chopped, plus more for garnish
- ½ teaspoon salt
- ½ teaspoon freshly ground black pepper
- 1 pound extra-large raw wild caught shrimp, 16-25 count, peeled and deveined
- lime wedges, to garnish

DIRECTIONS

In a medium bowl, whisk together olive oil, lime zest, garlic, chives, dill, mint, salt, and pepper until combined. Add the shrimp and stir to coat in the marinade. Cover and refrigerate at least 30 minutes or up to 2 hours.

Meanwhile, if using wooden skewers, soak the skewers in water for at least 30 minutes.

After marinating, divide shrimp evenly among the 8 skewers.

Preheat a grill or grill pan to medium and oil the grill. Grill the shrimp, flipping halfway through cooking, until curled and opaque, 5 to 8 minutes total.

Divide among plates and top each with more fresh herbs and serve with lime wedges. Serve immediately.

NUTRITION FACTS
Amount per serving | Calories 416 | Total Fat 17g | Saturated Fat 3.1g | Cholesterol 537mg | Sodium 914mg | Total Carbohydrate 5.1g | Dietary Fiber 0.5g | Total Sugars 0.1g | Protein 58.4g

KALE AND ARUGULA SALAD
WITH AVOCADO AND WALNUTS

PREP
15 MIN

COOK
15 MIN

SERVES
4

I like using curly kale for kale salads—the lacy edges of the leaves hold on to dressing better than the flat leaves of lacinato kale (also known as dinosaur or tuscan kale). Extra virgin olive oil and walnuts are great sources of polyphenols, the antioxidant phytonutrients in plants that help heal the gut and prevent long-term complications from diseases. Polyphenols are great for you, and you cannot get too much of them. The more, the better.

INGREDIENTS

- ¼ cup avocado oil mayonnaise

- 1 clove garlic, peeled and minced

- 2 tablespoons fresh lemon juice

- 2 tablespoons extra virgin olive oil

- 2 tablespoons water

- ½ teaspoon salt

- ½ teaspoon freshly ground black pepper

- 4 cups baby kale, washed

- 4 cups baby arugula, washed

- ¾ cup raw walnut halves

- 1 large avocado, halved, pitted, peeled, and sliced

DIRECTIONS

In a large bowl, whisk together mayonnaise, garlic, lemon juice, olive oil, water, salt, and pepper until smooth.

Add kale and arugula and toss until well coated with dressing.

Divide salad between 4 plates and top each with equal amounts of walnuts and avocado slices. Serve immediately.

NUTRITION FACTS
Amount per serving | Calories 328 | Total Fat 31.8g | Saturated Fat 4.2g | Cholesterol 20mg | Sodium 447mg | Total Carbohydrate 9.6g | Dietary Fiber 6.8g | Total Sugars 0.9g | Protein 4.5g

SHIITAKE SALMON SALAD

For lunch almost every day, I have a large salad with lots of veggies, protein, and a lot of high-phenolic extra virgin olive oil—about four tablespoons! I actually crave salads with high-phenolic olive oil. This salad provides a boost of health benefits from wild salmon, wild mushrooms, and ginger (which aid in digestion if you are prone to acid reflux).

PREP
15 MIN

MARINATE
3 HR

SERVES
4

INGREDIENTS

— 4 fillets wild caught salmon, center-cut, 4 to 6 oz. each

— 12 shiitake mushrooms, cleaned and stems discarded

— 4 cloves garlic, peeled and gently smashed

— 3 teaspoons fresh ginger, peeled, freshly grated, divided

— 10 tablespoons extra virgin olive oil, divided, plus more for brushing

— 2 teaspoons salt, divided

— 1 ½ teaspoons freshly ground black pepper, divided

— 2 tablespoons fresh lemon juice

— 4 cups butter lettuce, washed and torn

— 2 cups romaine lettuce, washed and torn

— 2 cups red leaf lettuce, washed and torn

— 4 radishes, washed and thinly sliced

DIRECTIONS

Have 2 gallon-size resealable bags ready. Place the salmon fillets in one bag and the mushrooms in the other.

Place 2 cloves of garlic, 1 teaspoon ginger, 2 tablespoons olive oil, ½ teaspoon salt, and ½ teaspoon pepper into the bag of salmon. Seal the bag and gently shake or massage to coat the salmon in the marinade. Repeat this process with the bag of mushrooms. Refrigerate the salmon and mushrooms for at least 1 hour or up to 3 hours. Remove the salmon and mushrooms from the refrigerator and let them come up to room temperature, about 20 minutes.

Meanwhile, in a small bowl, whisk together the lemon juice, remaining 1 teaspoon ginger, 6 tablespoons olive oil, 1 teaspoon salt, and ½ teaspoon pepper and set aside.

Preheat a grill or grill pan to medium-high heat and lightly oil the grill. Add the mushrooms to the grill and grill until warmed through and grill marks form, 4 to 6 minutes. Set aside. Add the salmon to the grill and cook until opaque and grill marks form on both sides, 4 to 6 minutes per side. Set aside.

In a large bowl, combine all the lettuces and radishes. Pour the dressing over the mixture and use tongs to toss and coat in the dressing. Divide the lettuce mixture evenly among 4 plates and top each with three mushrooms and a piece of salmon. Serve immediately.

NUTRITION FACTS
Amount per serving | Calories 637 | Total Fat 36.5g | Saturated Fat 5.4g | Cholesterol 177mg | Sodium 547mg | Total Carbohydrate 6.9g | Dietary Fiber 1.5g | Total Sugars 1.6g | Protein 69.6g

SEAWEED SALAD

PREP
20 MIN

SERVES
4

This flavorful sushi bar favorite is easy to make at home without all the added sugar. Seaweed is lectin free and rich in prebiotic fiber, making it a great choice for your gut. It's also a good source of methionine, an essential amino acid that helps metabolize fat and improves digestion. This salad would pair well with ginger garlic salmon and some cauliflower "fried" rice.

INGREDIENTS

- ¼ cup dried wakame seaweed (about 2 ounces)
- 3 cups filtered water
- ¼ cup toasted sesame oil
- 3 tablespoons white sesame seeds, toasted
- 2 tablespoons unseasoned rice vinegar
- 2 teaspoons fresh ginger, peeled and grated
- 1 teaspoon salt
- 1 lemon, sliced, for serving

DIRECTIONS

Place the wakame in a medium bowl and cover with 3 cups of filtered water. Let sit at room temperature until reconstituted, about 10 minutes. Drain well and return to the bowl. Set aside.

Meanwhile, in a small bowl, whisk together the sesame oil, sesame seeds, vinegar, ginger, and salt. Pour the dressing over the seaweed and toss until completely coated. Garnish with lemon wedges to serve.

NUTRITION FACTS
Amount per serving | Calories 188 | Total Fat 17.1g | Saturated Fat 2.4g | Cholesterol 0mg | Sodium 635mg | Total Carbohydrate 7.2g | Dietary Fiber 4.5g | Total Sugars 0.6g | Protein 2g

ALMOND EGGS ON A WILD HERB SALAD
WITH SMOKED SALMON

I bet you've never had eggs like this before! While I love a simple hard-boiled egg atop a salad, it's also fun to mix things up—like this recipe for boiled eggs pan-fried in a flavorful and crunchy almond coating. I like to pair these decadent almond eggs with wild greens, which are absolute nutritional powerhouses, rich in polyphenols and antioxidants.

PREP
10 MIN

COOK
35 MIN

SERVES
4

INGREDIENTS

- 5 large eggs, organic free-range
- 4 cups avocado oil
- 2 tablespoons arrowroot powder
- 1 ¼ cups cassava flour
- ¾ cup blanched almonds, chopped
- 4 slices smoked salmon, approx. 4 oz.
- 6 cups wild greens, washed and dried (e.g., dandelion leaves, wild garlic, sorrel, wild mint, etc.)
- 1 lemon, cut into wedges
- ½ teaspoon kosher salt
- ½ teaspoon freshly ground pepper

DIRECTIONS

Place four of the eggs in a large saucepan, add enough water to cover eggs with at least 1 inch of water and cover the pan. Bring to a boil. Remove pan from heat, keep covered, and allow to sit for 7 minutes. Drain well and refresh immediately in iced water.

Heat the oil in a large, heavy-based saucepan to 350°F. There should be at least 3 or 4 inches of oil throughout the pan.

Peel the eggs and rinse off any shell. Beat the remaining egg in a small bowl and add salt and freshly ground black pepper.

In another shallow bowl toss together the arrowroot powder, cassava flour, and chopped almonds.

Dip the cooked eggs into the beaten egg, let the excess drip off, and then coat in the cassava mixture. Fry in the hot oil for 3 to 4 minutes or until golden brown. Remove with a slotted spoon and drain on paper towels.

Arrange the wild leaves and herbs in bowls. Cut the eggs in half and place them on top, served with smoked salmon and lemon wedges.

NUTRITION FACTS
Amount per serving | Calories 424 | Total Fat 29.3g | Saturated Fat 4.4g | Cholesterol 206mg | Sodium 2092mg | Total Carbohydrate 16.3g | Dietary Fiber 3.4g | Total Sugars 2.2g | Protein 25.4g

BAKED GINGER AND SHALLOT SALMON AND BOK CHOY

PREP
15 MIN

COOK
15 MIN

SERVES
4

The zesty, Asian-inspired flavors of this filling one pan meal transform lunchtime into a vacation for the senses in 30 minutes or less. Wild Alaskan salmon is one of my favorite proteins—it's low in mercury and absolutely delicious.

INGREDIENTS

- 4 fresh wild caught salmon fillets, bones and skin removed, approx. 6 to 8 oz. each
- 1 pound baby bok choy, washed, trimmed, and halved lengthwise
- 1 shallot, peeled and thinly sliced
- 2 cloves garlic, peeled and thinly sliced
- 1 tablespoon fresh ginger, peeled and grated
- 1 tablespoon fresh lime zest
- 2 tablespoons fresh lime juice
- ¼ cup extra virgin olive oil
- 1 ¼ teaspoons salt
- 1 teaspoon freshly ground black pepper
- 1 cup fresh cilantro sprigs
- ¼ cup fresh mint leaves
- 1 lime, cut into wedges, for serving

DIRECTIONS

Preheat oven to 350°F.

Arrange the salmon and bok choy in a shallow baking dish. Scatter the shallot, garlic, ginger, and lime zest over the top. Drizzle with lime juice and olive oil and sprinkle all over with salt and pepper. Cover the baking dish with tin foil.

Bake the salmon until firm to the touch and opaque in appearance, 12 to 15 minutes.

Remove the foil from the baking dish and garnish the salmon with cilantro springs, mint leaves, and lime wedges. Serve immediately.

NUTRITION FACTS

Amount per serving | Calories 443 | Total Fat 26.8g | Saturated Fat 3.9g | Cholesterol 98mg | Sodium 908mg | Total Carbohydrate 8.7g | Dietary Fiber 2.6g | Total Sugars 1.9g | Protein 45.9g

BEEF WITH CHINESE BROCCOLI AND ALMONDS

Savory and satisfying, this takeout-inspired meal comes together faster than ordering from your favorite Chinese food restaurant. The sauce is a clever combination of flavorful gut-friendly ingredients, like probiotic miso, prebiotic garlic, and polyphenol-rich ginger. (Be sure to choose grass-fed and organic steak to avoid the gut damaging effects of meat fed a diet of corn, soy, or wheat.)

PREP
10 MIN

COOK
15 MIN

SERVES
4

INGREDIENTS

— 1 pound sirloin steak, thinly sliced against grain

— 3 tablespoons coconut aminos, divided

— 3 tablespoons avocado oil, divided

— 1 teaspoon miso paste

— 2 teaspoons fish sauce

— ¼ cup beef stock

— 3 tablespoons rice vinegar

— 1 clove garlic, peeled and minced

— ½-inch piece of ginger root, peeled and minced

— ½ pound Chinese broccoli, trimmed and cut into sections (about 3 cups)

— ½ teaspoon kosher salt, or more to taste

— ½ teaspoon freshly ground black pepper, or more to taste

— 4 tablespoons slivered almonds, toasted

— 1 lime, cut into quarters

DIRECTIONS

Place steak in a medium bowl and season with one tablespoon coconut aminos, one tablespoon avocado oil, and the miso paste. Thoroughly coat and set aside.

In a small bowl, whisk remaining coconut aminos with fish sauce, beef stock, vinegar, garlic, and ginger.

Heat one tablespoon avocado oil in a large wok or frying pan set over high heat. Add Chinese broccoli and stir fry until tender, about 3 minutes. Remove from the wok to a bowl. set aside.

Add remaining oil to the wok. Cook the steak in a single layer undisturbed until it browns, about 2 to 3 minutes. Turn the steak and add broccoli and the prepared sauce to the wok.

Bring the dish to a boil, cooking until the sauce has thickened, about 2 to 3 minutes. Season with salt and pepper.

Serve straight from wok, garnish with almonds, and serve with lime wedges for squeezing.

NUTRITION FACTS
Amount per serving | Calories 331 | Total Fat 14g | Saturated Fat 3.3g | Cholesterol 101mg | Sodium 735mg | Total Carbohydrate 10.9g | Dietary Fiber 3.2g | Total Sugars 1.9g | Protein 38.3g

DANDELION SALAD
WITH PINE NUTS IN LEMON DRESSING

PREP
15 MIN

COOK
15 MIN

SERVES
4

You will be eating a lot of salads on your gut-healing journey, so mix things up by trying a wide range of greens beyond romaine and iceberg lettuce. Wild greens like dandelion leaves are a great source of prebiotics, vitamins, and minerals, and have even been used in traditional medicine to support the liver.

INGREDIENTS

- 6 tablespoons extra virgin olive oil
- 2 tablespoons fresh lemon juice
- 1 teaspoon salt
- 1 teaspoon freshly ground black pepper
- 2 cups dandelion leaves, washed and trimmed
- 4 cups butter lettuce
- 1 cup beet sprouts
- ½ cup raw pine nuts

DIRECTIONS

In a large bowl, whisk together the olive oil, lemon juice, salt, and pepper.

Add the dandelion greens, lettuce, sprouts, and nuts. Toss gently until well coated. Serve immediately.

NUTRITION FACTS

Amount per serving | Calories 322 | Total Fat 33.2g | Saturated Fat 4g | Cholesterol 0mg | Sodium 608mg | Total Carbohydrate 7.2g | Dietary Fiber 2.1g | Total Sugars 1.5g | Protein 3.8g

GARLIC AND GINGER CHICKEN STIR FRY WITH ASPARAGUS, SHIITAKE MUSHROOMS, AND SPINACH

Think of this quick and easy stir fry as a template for a whole host of lunchtime variations. Experiment with different greens and vegetables like bok choy, carrots, broccoli, or cauliflower to bring healthy variety to your plate. Remember, when shopping for chicken, look for pastured, organic, or free-range (not soy or corn fed).

PREP
10 MIN

COOK
20 MIN

SERVES
4

INGREDIENTS

- 2 boneless, skinless, organic free-range chicken breasts, approx. 4 to 6 oz. each, cut into 1-inch pieces
- 3 tablespoons extra virgin olive oil, divided
- 1 ½ teaspoons salt, divided
- 1 teaspoon freshly ground black pepper
- 2 tablespoons arrowroot powder
- ¼ cup chicken broth, organic free-range
- 4 cloves garlic, peeled and finely chopped
- 2 teaspoons fresh ginger, peeled and grated
- ½ pound shiitake mushrooms, stems removed caps sliced thin
- 1 pound thin asparagus, washed, ends trimmed, cut into 1-inch pieces
- 5 cups baby spinach, washed and dried
- ¼ cup scallions, washed and thinly sliced

DIRECTIONS

In a medium bowl, combine chicken, 1 tablespoon olive oil, 1 teaspoon each of salt and pepper.

In another small bowl, whisk together the arrowroot, chicken broth, and remaining ½ teaspoon salt. Set aside.

In a large skillet, heat 2 remaining tablespoons of olive oil over medium-high heat. Add the chicken to the skillet and cook, flipping once or twice, until it is golden brown in parts and cooked through, 6 to 9 minutes. Transfer the chicken to a plate.

Add garlic and ginger to the skillet and cook, stirring constantly, until fragrant, about 1 minute. Add mushrooms and asparagus and cook, stirring occasionally, until cooked through, 4 to 6 minutes.

Add the spinach to the skillet and cook, stirring occasionally, until just wilted. Add the chicken back to the skillet and cook until heated through.

Add the arrowroot mixture to the skillet, bring to a boil, and cook until slightly thickened, 2 to 3 minutes. Stir in the scallions and serve immediately.

NUTRITION FACTS
Amount per serving | Calories 288 | Total Fat 11.4g | Saturated Fat 1.2g | Cholesterol 69mg | Sodium 1503mg | Total Carbohydrate 16.6g | Dietary Fiber 4.9g | Total Sugars 4.6g | Protein 32.8g

GRILLED CHICKEN, RADISH, CELERY, AND CABBAGE SALAD

PREP
25 MIN

COOK
12 MIN

SERVES
4

If you like your chicken salad with a lot of crunch, you'll love this recipe loaded with prebiotic-rich radishes and gut-friendly celery. I like using a blend of red and savoy cabbage for color and variety, but feel free to substitute green cabbage or even a pre-shredded organic coleslaw mix to cut down on prep time.

INGREDIENTS

- 4 boneless, skinless, organic free-range chicken breasts, approx. 5 to 8 oz. each
- 8 tablespoons extra virgin olive oil, divided
- 2 teaspoons salt
- 1 ½ teaspoons freshly ground black pepper
- ¼ cup fresh lemon juice
- 1 clove garlic, peeled and minced
- 4 radishes, cleaned, trimmed, and thinly sliced
- 2 stalks celery, cleaned, ends trimmed and sliced into ½-inch pieces
- ½ small red onion, peeled and thinly sliced
- 4 cups savoy cabbage, thinly sliced
- 4 cups red cabbage, thinly sliced

DIRECTIONS

Pat the chicken dry with paper towels and place in a shallow baking dish. Drizzle the chicken all over with 4 tablespoons olive oil, and season with 1 teaspoon salt and 1 teaspoon pepper. Toss to coat well in the seasoning.

Preheat a grill or grill pan to medium-high heat and grill the chicken, flipping halfway through cooking, until grill marks form and the chicken is cooked through, 9 to 12 minutes. Transfer to a cutting board to rest for about 5 minutes before slicing the chicken into 1-inch pieces.

In a large bowl, whisk together the lemon juice, garlic, remaining 4 tablespoons olive oil, 1 teaspoon salt, and ½ teaspoon pepper. Add the radishes, celery, onion, and both cabbages and toss well to combine.

Divide the salad evenly between 4 bowls and top each with a chopped chicken breast. Serve immediately.

NUTRITION FACTS

Amount per serving | Calories 418 | Total Fat 23.1g | Saturated Fat 2.7g | Cholesterol 96mg | Sodium 1785mg | Total Carbohydrate 12.9g | Dietary Fiber 5.4g | Total Sugars 6.8g | Protein 41.4g

GRILLED LEMON, HERB, AND GARLIC TUNA STEAKS

Herbs and garlic are the superheroes of a gut-friendly diet: low in calories but sky-high in flavor and nutrients. Exploring the wide range of nature's whole food seasonings is a great way to avoid mealtime boredom. In this recipe I use parsley and basil, along with fresh garlic, but feel free to experiment with other fresh herbs like oregano or thyme.

PREP
10 MIN

MARINATE
10 MIN

COOK
30 MIN

SERVES
4

INGREDIENTS

— 4 wild caught tuna steaks, bones and skin removed, sliced 1 inch thick (approx. 4 to 6 oz. each)

— 3 tablespoons extra virgin olive oil, plus more for the grill and drizzling

— 1 tablespoon fresh lemon zest

— 1 teaspoon fresh lemon juice

— 1 teaspoon fresh oregano, finely chopped

— 1 clove garlic, peeled and minced

— 1 teaspoon salt

— 1 teaspoon freshly cracked black pepper

— ¼ cup fresh flat-leaf parsley leaves

— ¼ cup fresh basil leaves, torn

— 1 lemon, cut into wedges, for serving

DIRECTIONS

Place the tuna steaks in a shallow baking dish.

In a small bowl, combine the olive oil, lemon zest, lemon juice, oregano, garlic, salt, and pepper. Pour the marinade over the tuna steaks and let stand about 10 minutes to allow the flavors to absorb.

Meanwhile, preheat a grill or grill pan to medium-high heat.

Brush the grill with oil. Grill the tuna until seared on the outside and slightly pink on the inside, 2 to 5 minutes per side.

Transfer the tuna to a serving platter and top with parsley and basil and drizzle with more oil. Serve with lemon wedges. Serve warm or at room temperature.

NUTRITION FACTS

Amount per serving | Calories 308 | Total Fat 15.2g | Saturated Fat 3.1g | Cholesterol 62mg | Sodium 648mg | Total Carbohydrate 3.8g | Dietary Fiber 1.3g | Total Sugars 0.8g | Protein 38.8g

GRILLED TUNA SKEWERS
WITH ASPARAGUS AND SCALLIONS

PREP
30 MIN

COOK
6 MIN

SERVES
4

Grilling healthy ingredients on skewers is an easy way to make simple ingredients feel special. The meatiness of wild tuna steaks offers a fun and surprising alternative to beef or chicken kebabs, especially if you're used to tuna out of a can.

INGREDIENTS

— 8 wooden or metal skewers

— 1 ¼ pounds wild caught tuna steak, bones and skin removed, cut into 1 ½-inch cubes

— 1 tablespoon fresh lemon zest

— 1 tablespoon fresh lemon juice

— 1 tablespoon fresh flat-leaf parsley, finely chopped

— 1 tablespoon fresh thyme leaves, finely chopped

— 1 teaspoon fresh oregano leaves, finely chopped

— 1 teaspoon fresh rosemary leaves, finely chopped

— ¼ cup extra virgin olive oil, plus more for grill

— 1 ½ teaspoons salt

— 1 teaspoon freshly ground black pepper

— 1 pound asparagus, thick ends trimmed, sliced into 2-inch pieces

— 1 bunch scallions, ends trimmed and sliced into 2-inch pieces

— 1 lemon, cut into wedges, for serving

DIRECTIONS

If using wooden skewers, place them in a shallow baking dish and soak in water for about 30 minutes before grilling.

Meanwhile, in a medium bowl, combine tuna with the lemon zest, lemon juice, parsley, thyme, oregano, rosemary, olive oil, salt, and pepper and toss to coat well in the marinade.

Thread the tuna, asparagus, and scallions evenly among the 8 skewers.

Preheat a grill or grill pan to medium-high heat and oil the grates of the grill.

Add the skewers to the hot grill, and cook, turning occasionally, until the tuna is seared on the outside and slightly pink in the middle and the asparagus and scallions are heated through, 6 to 8 minutes total. Transfer the skewers to a serving platter or four plates and garnish with lemon wedges. Serve immediately.

NUTRITION FACTS
*Amount per serving | Calories 298 |
Total Fat 14.1g | Saturated Fat 2.9g |
Cholesterol 52mg | Sodium 933mg |
Total Carbohydrate 9.5g | Dietary Fiber 4.3g |
Total Sugars 3.3g | Protein 35.1g*

LETTUCE CUPS WITH CHICKEN, CARROTS, AND SESAME SEEDS

PREP
25 MIN

A popular appetizer at Asian restaurants, chicken lettuce cups are a quick, easy, and healthy meal with a fun hands-on element. Experiment with different kinds of lettuce for the wraps—butter lettuce, green leaf lettuce, iceberg, and romaine are popular choices, but endive or cabbage leaves are great too. Make a double batch for two days' worth of lunches but be sure to store the lettuce leaves separately. (They'll get soggy if stored with the savory chicken filling.)

COOK
30 MIN

SERVES
4

INGREDIENTS

— 4 boneless, skinless, organic free-range chicken breasts

— ½ teaspoon kosher salt

— ¼ teaspoon freshly ground black pepper

— 2 tablespoons avocado oil

— 1 onion, peeled and sliced

— 2 cloves garlic, peeled and minced

— ½ cup water chestnuts

— 3 tablespoons coconut aminos

— 1 tablespoon lime juice

— 4 scallions

— 2 Boston lettuce heads

— 2 medium carrots

— 2 tablespoons sesame seeds, toasted

DIRECTIONS

Preheat oven to 375ºF. Season chicken with salt and pepper. Roast the chicken breasts in a baking dish for 20 to 30 minutes. Allow to cool, then cut into bite-sized pieces.

Meanwhile, heat avocado oil in a small skillet over medium heat and cook the onion and garlic for 2 to 3 minutes, or until the onion begins to turn golden. Add the water chestnuts, coconut aminos, and lime juice, and cook for 1 minute or until warmed through. Remove from heat.

Place the chicken and scallions into a large bowl. Add the onion and water chestnut mixture and gently toss.

Separate the lettuce leaves and divide them among four plates (about 4 per plate). Fill with the chicken mixture and top with sliced carrots and sesame seeds. Serve immediately.

NUTRITION FACTS
Amount per serving | Calories 337 | Total Fat 11.7g | Saturated Fat 1.1g | Cholesterol 98mg | Sodium 470mg | Total Carbohydrate 16.2g | Dietary Fiber 4.3g | Total Sugars 6.8g | Protein 42.7g

LUMP CRAB CHOPPED SALAD WITH SAFFRON VINAIGRETTE

PREP
20 MIN

COOK
20 MIN

SERVES
4

This recipe is packed with gut-friendly ingredients, from the polyphenol-packed wild dandelion greens and prebiotic-rich asparagus and radishes to my favorite "fruit"—avocado! If you don't have crab, try this recipe with cooked salmon or even leftover chicken. It's the unique saffron dressing that makes it truly special.

INGREDIENTS

VINAIGRETTE

- 3 tablespoons lemon juice
- 5 tablespoons extra virgin olive oil
- 1 small clove garlic, peeled and grated
- 1 teaspoon Dijon mustard
- 2 pinches saffron threads
- ½ teaspoon kosher salt, or more to taste
- ½ teaspoon freshly ground pepper, or more to taste

CHOPPED SALAD

- 1 pound fresh lump crab meat
- 2 tablespoons fresh chives, finely chopped, divided
- 1 tablespoon unsweetened coconut yogurt
- ¼ cup celery, washed and finely chopped
- ¼ cup red radish, washed and chopped
- ½ cup carrots, washed, peeled, and grated
- ½ cup cooked asparagus, chopped

- ½ cup avocado, halved, peeled, seeded, and cubed
- 1 cup dandelion greens, washed and sliced chiffonade
- 1 head romaine lettuce, washed and chopped
- 1 green onion, thinly sliced
- ½ teaspoon kosher salt, or more to taste
- ½ teaspoon freshly ground pepper, or more to taste

DIRECTIONS

For the vinaigrette: Combine all the ingredients in a small bowl and mix well.

For the chopped salad: In a separate bowl, mix ⅛ cup of the vinaigrette with the crab meat, one tablespoon fresh chives, and unsweetened coconut yogurt. Add ½ teaspoon each of salt and pepper.

In a large salad bowl, combine the remaining ingredients and drizzle with the remaining dressing. Spoon the crab mix over the top of the salad and garnish with the remaining chives.

NUTRITION FACTS

*Amount per serving | Calories 262 |
Total Fat 25.5g | Saturated Fat 3.6g |
Cholesterol 26mg | Sodium 903mg |
Total Carbohydrate 10.4g | Dietary Fiber 3.8g |
Total Sugars 2.8g | Protein 8.8g*

48

MINI CHICKEN BURGERS
OVER ARUGULA SALAD

PREP
20 MIN

COOK
10 MIN

SERVES
4

It's burger time! I like adding gut-friendly shredded carrots to my chicken burgers to boost the colorful vegetable content of the meal. Carrots are low in FODMAPs, making this a good option for someone looking to avoid ingredients that cause gas and bloating (just be sure to leave out the garlic).

INGREDIENTS

BURGERS
- 1 ½ pounds ground chicken, organic free-range
- 1 medium carrot, peeled and finely grated
- 2 cloves garlic, peeled and minced
- 1 teaspoon dried thyme
- 1 teaspoon salt
- 1 teaspoon freshly ground black pepper
- 1 large egg, organic free-range, lightly beaten
- 2 tablespoons extra virgin olive oil

SALAD
- ¼ cup fresh lime juice
- 6 tablespoons extra virgin olive oil
- ½ teaspoon salt
- ½ teaspoon freshly cracked black pepper
- 8 cups baby arugula, washed and dried
- 1 lime, cut into wedges, for garnish

DIRECTIONS

For the burgers: In a large bowl, combine ground chicken, carrot, garlic, thyme, salt, pepper, and egg. Using your hands, divide and form the mixture into approximately 12 2-inch mini patties.

In a large heavy-bottomed skillet, heat olive oil over medium heat. Cook the patties until the chicken is cooked through and no longer pink, 4 to 6 minutes per side.

For the salad: In a large bowl, whisk together lime juice, olive oil, salt, and pepper. Add the arugula and toss well to combine. Divide the salad between 4 bowls and top each with the mini chicken burgers. Garnish with wedges of lime and serve immediately.

NUTRITION FACTS
Amount per serving | Calories 380 | Total Fat 31.5g | Saturated Fat 6g | Cholesterol 143mg | Sodium 974mg | Total Carbohydrate 5.5g | Dietary Fiber 1.5g | Total Sugars 1.6g | Protein 22.1g

MINI HERB AND MUSHROOM FRITTATAS

PREP
10 MIN

COOK
25 MIN

SERVES
6

Who said frittatas are just for breakfast? I love filling these mini crustless quiches with a wide variety of greens and fresh herbs, but you can also toss in dinner leftovers for an easy and delicious fridge cleanup. These freeze well, so feel free to make a double batch and store in the freezer for an easy grab-and-go meal. Simply pop them in the microwave for 30 second increments until heated through.

INGREDIENTS

- Avocado oil cooking spray
- 2 tablespoons extra virgin olive oil
- 2 cups cremini mushrooms, cleaned and quartered
- 2 shallots, finely chopped
- ½ teaspoon kosher salt, divided, or more to taste
- ½ teaspoon freshly ground black pepper, divided, or more to taste
- 12 large eggs
- ⅔ cup unsweetened almond milk
- 2 teaspoons miso paste
- 2 cups fresh spinach leaves, clean and roughly chopped
- 2 tablespoons fresh dill, finely chopped
- 2 tablespoons fresh parsley, finely chopped
- 2 tablespoons fresh chives, finely chopped
- 1 medium carrot, cleaned and finely grated

DIRECTIONS

Preheat oven to 350°F. Spray a 12-cup muffin pan with avocado oil cooking spray.

In a skillet, heat the olive oil over moderate heat until hot. Add the mushrooms and shallots plus about half of the salt and pepper. Sauté 5 minutes and set aside.

In a large mixing bowl, thoroughly beat together the eggs, almond milk, miso paste, spinach, dill, parsley, chives, and carrot, plus remaining salt and pepper. Then, add the mushroom and shallot mixture.

Ladle frittata mix into the prepared muffin pan.

Bake until the frittatas rise, set, and are golden (about 15 to 20 minutes).

Remove from the oven and let them cool briefly before turning out to serve.

NUTRITION FACTS
*Amount per serving | Calories 213 |
Total Fat 15.3g | Saturated Fat 3.8g |
Cholesterol 372mg | Sodium 445mg |
Total Carbohydrate 5.8g | Dietary Fiber 1.1g |
Total Sugars 1.9g | Protein 14.4g*

OVEN-BAKED SWEET POTATO LATKES WITH KEFIR DILL SAUCE

These colorful sweet potato pancakes combine Eastern European and Scandinavian flavors for a lunch packed with gut-healing carbs and fresh herbs. These would be excellent served with smoked salmon or topped with fried eggs for brunch.

PREP
15 MIN

COOK
40 MIN

SERVES
4

INGREDIENTS

KEFIR DILL SAUCE

- ½ cup unsweetened coconut yogurt
- ¼ cup unsweetened kefir
- 2 tablespoons dill, finely chopped
- 2 tablespoons green onion, finely chopped
- 1 teaspoon fresh lemon juice
- 1 teaspoon lemon zest
- ½ teaspoon kosher salt, or more to taste
- 1 ¼ teaspoons pink peppercorns, crushed, divided
- 1 teaspoon olive oil, for garnish

LATKES

- 4 medium sweet potatoes, peeled and shredded
- 1 medium yellow onion, peeled and shredded
- 2 large eggs
- 2 teaspoons kosher salt
- 2 teaspoons baking powder
- ¼ cup coconut flour
- 1 teaspoon ground chia seed flour
- ¾ cup avocado oil

NUTRITION FACTS
Amount per serving | Calories 484 |
Total Fat 23.1g | Saturated Fat 5.6g |
Cholesterol 95mg | Sodium 1555mg |
Total Carbohydrate 62.7g | Dietary Fiber 15.6g |
Total Sugars 5.5g | Protein 9.8g

DIRECTIONS

For the kefir dill sauce: Combine the coconut yogurt, kefir, dill, green onion, lemon juice, lemon zest, salt, and one teaspoon of pink peppercorns in a bowl. Cover and refrigerate until the latkes are ready to serve.

For the sweet potato latkes: Preheat the oven to 425°F.

Combine the sweet potato and onion in a bowl and let sit for 15 minutes. Place the mixture in a fine sieve over a bowl or sink and press down with a paper towel, releasing any juices.

Mix the sweet potato and onion mixture with the eggs, salt, baking powder, coconut flour, and chia seed flour.

Brush equal amounts of avocado oil onto two non-stick baking sheets and heat in the oven for ten minutes. Then, divide the batter between the heated pans into approximately 20 individual pancake rounds. Use the back of a measuring cup to press down and flatten each latke.

Bake for fifteen to twenty minutes or until the bottom of the latkes are golden. Flip the latkes and bake for ten minutes on the other side.

Remove from the oven and serve immediately with the kefir dill sauce topped with the remaining pink peppercorn and a drizzle of olive oil.

51

ROASTED ASPARAGUS
WITH CITRUS VINAIGRETTE

PREP
10 MIN

COOK
20 MIN

SERVES
2

It's amazing what a tangy vinaigrette can do for simply prepared vegetables. This zesty, orange-infused dressing is an excellent drizzle for all sorts of roasted vegetables and would be equally delicious on roasted carrots or radishes. (Asparagus are on the EWG's Clean Fifteen list of produce with the lowest amount of pesticide residue, so feel free to purchase non-organic asparagus for this dish.)

INGREDIENTS

- 12 asparagus spears, woody ends trimmed
- 2 ½ tablespoons extra virgin olive oil, divided
- ½ teaspoon kosher salt, or more to taste
- ¼ teaspoon freshly ground black pepper, or more to taste
- 2 tablespoons fresh lemon juice
- 1 lemon, zested
- 2 tablespoons orange juice
- 1 teaspoon orange zest
- 1 teaspoon Dijon mustard
- ¼ cup fresh flat-leaf parsley, chopped

DIRECTIONS

Preheat oven to 425°F and line a baking sheet with parchment paper. Place the asparagus on the parchment and season with ½ tablespoon of olive oil plus salt and pepper.

Roast the asparagus for 15 to 20 minutes until they are bright green and fork tender.

While asparagus is roasting, prepare the vinaigrette. In a small bowl, combine the remaining olive oil, lemon juice, lemon zest, orange juice, orange zest, and Dijon mustard.

Place the cooked asparagus in a serving dish and spoon the dressing over the asparagus. Top with fresh parsley and serve immediately.

NUTRITION FACTS
Amount per serving | Calories 114 | Total Fat 7.6g | Saturated Fat 1.2g | Cholesterol 0mg | Sodium 621mg | Total Carbohydrate 11.2g | Dietary Fiber 4.4g | Total Sugars 5.1g | Protein 4.1g

ROASTED SWEET POTATO WEDGES
WITH GINGER AND LIME

Think of these as gut-friendly fries, swapping high-carb potatoes for healing sweet potatoes and loading up on superfoods like fresh herbs and ginger. These would make an excellent side dish for roasted chicken or salmon. For the best wedges, shop for small to medium sweet potatoes

PREP
10 MIN

COOK
45 MIN

SERVES
4

INGREDIENTS

- 2 pounds sweet potatoes, scrubbed and cut into ½-inch-thick wedges
- 2 tablespoons extra virgin olive oil
- 1 teaspoon salt
- ½ teaspoon freshly ground black pepper
- 3 tablespoons fresh flat-leaf parsley, finely chopped
- 3 tablespoons fresh mint leaves, finely chopped
- 1 teaspoon fresh ginger, peeled and grated
- 1 lime, cut into wedges, for serving

DIRECTIONS

Preheat oven to 425°F. Line a baking sheet with parchment paper.

Spread sweet potato wedges on the baking sheet, drizzle with olive oil, and season with salt and pepper. Roast the sweet potatoes, flipping once during cooking, until golden brown in spots and cooked through, 35 to 45 minutes.

Remove from the oven and transfer the wedges to a serving plate. Sprinkle the sweet potatoes with parsley, mint, and ginger and serve with lime wedges.

NUTRITION FACTS

Amount per serving | Calories 338 | Total Fat 7.5g | Saturated Fat 1.1g | Cholesterol 0mg | Sodium 605mg | Total Carbohydrate 66g | Dietary Fiber 10.3g | Total Sugars 1.5g | Protein 3.9g

SALAD NIÇOISE WITH TUNA, EGG, AND OLIVES

**PREP
15 MIN**

**COOK
30 MIN**

**SERVES
4**

This classic French salad has it all—protein, greens, fiber, and healthy fats—and will transport you to a sidewalk cafe in Paris. Salad Niçoise is often served as a composed salad (with ingredients and dressing arranged on top of the greens) as opposed to a tossed salad, but I like to toss some of the ingredients to make sure the dressing is evenly spread over the vegetables, and arrange the tuna, egg, and olives on top.

INGREDIENTS

- 4 large eggs, organic free-range
- 4 tuna steaks, wild caught (approx.– 4 to 6 oz. each), bones and skin removed, sliced 1 inch thick
- ½ cup extra virgin olive oil, plus more for the grill
- 2 tablespoons fresh lemon juice
- 1 tablespoon fresh lemon zest
- 1 ½ teaspoons salt
- 1 ½ teaspoons freshly ground black pepper
- 1 head Boston lettuce, washed, dried, trimmed, with leaves separated
- 1 head radicchio, washed, dried, thinly sliced
- ½ small red onion, peeled and thinly sliced
- ½ cup black Niçoise olives, pitted

DIRECTIONS

Place eggs in a medium saucepan and cover with water by 1 inch, bring to a boil over high heat, and boil uncovered for 7 to 9 minutes. Drain the eggs and then run under cold water until cool enough to peel. Carefully peel, cut each egg in half lengthwise, and set aside.

Meanwhile, place the tuna steaks in a shallow baking dish.

In a small bowl, combine the olive oil, lemon juice, lemon zest, salt, and pepper.

Pour half of the dressing over the tuna steaks. Reserve the other half of the dressing. Use tongs or clean hands to gently coat the tuna steaks in the dressing and let stand about 10 minutes to allow the flavors to absorb.

Preheat a grill or grill pan to medium-high heat.

Brush the grill with oil. Grill the tuna until seared on the outside and slightly pink on the inside, 2 to 5 minutes per side. Transfer the tuna to a cutting board and let rest about 5 minutes.

In a large bowl, combine the lettuce, radicchio, and onion with the remaining dressing. Divide the salad evenly among 4 plates.

Slice the tuna steaks across the grain and place a sliced tuna steak on top of each salad. Arrange one sliced egg and some olives over the top of each plate. Serve immediately.

NUTRITION FACTS

Amount per serving | Calories 328 | Total Fat 23g | Saturated Fat 4.5g | Cholesterol 195mg | Sodium 687mg | Total Carbohydrate 5.9g | Dietary Fiber 1.5g | Total Sugars 1.8g | Protein 25.6g

SESAME CHICKEN SALAD

While this salad is reminiscent of Chinese chicken salads popularized at American restaurants in the 1990s, my spin on the recipe gives a gut friendly boost with fresh herbs and polyphenol-rich olive oil. To make it extra satisfying, add a few slices of avocado or top with crunchy roasted almonds.

PREP
20 MIN

MARINATE
20 MIN

COOK
12 MIN

SERVES
4

INGREDIENTS

- 4 boneless, skinless, organic free-range chicken breasts, approx. 6 oz. each
- 6 tablespoons toasted sesame oil, divided
- 2 teaspoons fresh ginger, peeled and grated
- 1 ¾ teaspoons salt, divided
- 1 ½ teaspoons freshly ground black pepper, divided
- 6 tablespoons extra virgin olive oil, divided
- 2 tablespoons unseasoned rice vinegar
- 1 garlic clove, peeled and minced
- 2 tablespoons toasted sesame seeds
- 12 cups romaine lettuce, washed, dried, and shredded (approx. 2 heads)
- 1 cup carrots, peeled and grated
- ½ cup fresh basil leaves
- ¼ cup scallions, washed and sliced
- ¼ cup fresh mint leaves

DIRECTIONS

Pat chicken dry with paper towels. Place chicken in a shallow baking dish.

In a small bowl, whisk together 3 tablespoons sesame oil, ginger, 1 teaspoon salt and 1 teaspoon pepper. Coat the chicken in the marinade and let stand about 20 minutes at room temperature to allow the flavors to absorb.

In a large heavy-bottomed skillet, heat 2 tablespoons olive oil over medium-high heat. Add the chicken breasts and cook, without moving, until the chicken breasts are seared on one side, 4 to 6 minutes. Flip the chicken and continue to cook without moving until seared on both sides and cooked through, 4 to 6 more minutes. Transfer chicken breasts to a cutting board and let rest about 10 minutes before cutting across the grain into ½-inch-thick slices.

Meanwhile, in a small bowl, whisk together the remaining 3 tablespoons sesame oil, 4 tablespoons olive oil, rice vinegar, garlic, sesame seeds, and the remaining salt and pepper. Set aside.

In a large bowl, combine the lettuce, carrots, basil, scallions, and mint. Add the dressing and toss well to combine. Divide the salad among 4 plates and top each with a sliced chicken breast. Serve immediately.

NUTRITION FACTS
Amount per serving | Calories 461 | Total Fat 36.6g | Saturated Fat 4.8g | Cholesterol 55mg | Sodium 1381mg | Total Carbohydrate 11.1g | Dietary Fiber 3.2g | Total Sugars 3.2g | Protein 24.4g

SOFT BOILED EGGS
WITH HERBS

PREP
10 MIN

COOK
20 MIN
CHILL
10 MIN

SERVES
4

This is a great recipe to have in your back pocket for those "what can I quickly make for lunch" days. Soft boiled eggs combine perfectly cooked whites with jammy, silky yolks for a luxe lunch that takes barely any time at all. The more herbs the merrier, so feel free to add tarragon, chervil, dill, or parsley.

INGREDIENTS

- 8 large eggs, organic free-range
- 2 tablespoons extra virgin olive oil
- ½ cup fresh cilantro, finely chopped
- 2 tablespoons fresh chives, snipped
- 1 teaspoon salt
- 1 teaspoon freshly ground black pepper

DIRECTIONS

In a large saucepan, cover the eggs with about 1 inch of cold water. Bring the water to a boil over high heat and cook for 1 minute.

Remove the saucepan from heat and cover it with a tight-fitting lid. Set aside for 4 minutes.

Immediately transfer the eggs to a large bowl of ice water until very cold, about 10 minutes. Drain, crack, and peel the eggs, rinsing off any shell.

Cut the eggs in half lengthwise and place on a serving platter. Drizzle the eggs with olive oil and sprinkle with cilantro, chives, salt, and pepper. Serve immediately or refrigerate and serve within a few hours.

NUTRITION FACTS
Amount per serving | Calories 205 | Total Fat 17g | Saturated Fat 4.1g | Cholesterol 372mg | Sodium 723mg | Total Carbohydrate | Dietary Fiber 0.2g | Total Sugars 0.8g | Protein 12.7g

SPINACH SALAD WITH GRILLED CHICKEN, MUSHROOMS, AND ONION

PREP
10 MIN

MARINATE
20 MIN

COOK
25 MIN

SERVES
4

Because this simple but flavorful salad is topped with fresh-off-the-grill chicken and veggies, it can feel more filling than a typical raw veggie salad. Spinach is notoriously high in pesticides (topping the EWG's Dirty Dozen list, along with strawberries) so be sure to shop for organic spinach.

INGREDIENTS

- 4 boneless, skinless, organic free-range chicken breasts, approx. 6 oz. each

- 1 large red onion, peeled, sliced into ½-inch-thick rounds

- ½ pound shiitake mushrooms, washed, stems removed

- ½ cup extra virgin olive oil, divided

- 2 teaspoons salt, divided

- 1 ½ teaspoons freshly ground black pepper, divided

- 2 tablespoons fresh oregano, chopped

- 2 tablespoons red wine vinegar

- 3 cups baby spinach leaves, washed and dried

DIRECTIONS

Pat chicken dry with paper towels. Place the chicken in a shallow baking dish and the onions and mushrooms in a separate shallow baking dish. Drizzle the chicken with 2 tablespoons olive oil and season with 1 teaspoon salt and ½ teaspoon pepper. Drizzle the onions and mushrooms with 2 tablespoons olive oil and season with ½ teaspoon salt and ½ teaspoon pepper. Let the chicken, onion, and mushrooms sit out at room temperature about 20 minutes.

Meanwhile, preheat a grill or grill pan to medium-high heat. Oil the grates of the grill.

Grill the onions and mushrooms, flipping halfway through cooking until heated through and grill marks form, about 3 to 5 minutes per side. Transfer the vegetables to a cutting board to cool slightly while grilling the chicken.

Grill the chicken until grill marks form and the chicken reads an internal temperature of 165°F, 5 to 8 minutes per side. Transfer the chicken to the cutting board with the vegetables and let rest 5 minutes before slicing the chicken and vegetables into 1-inch pieces.

In a large bowl, whisk together the remaining ¼ cup olive oil, oregano, vinegar, ½ teaspoon salt, and ½ teaspoon pepper. Add the chopped chicken, onions, mushrooms, and spinach to the dressing and toss well. Divide the salad among 4 plates and serve immediately.

NUTRITION FACTS

Amount per serving | Calories 361 | Total Fat 19g | Saturated Fat 2.1g | Cholesterol 83mg | Sodium 1233mg | Total Carbohydrate 14.2g | Dietary Fiber 3.7g | Total Sugars 3.9g | Protein 35.3g

STEAMED CLAMS
WITH CHIMICHURRI AND LEMON

PREP
20 MIN

SOAK
2 HR

COOK
7 MIN

SERVES
4

Chimichurri is a traditional Argentinean sauce made with parsley and garlic—a bit like a South American pesto—that is excellent with all kinds of protein and vegetables. In this recipe, it's drizzled over steamed clams for a flavorful, protein-packed meal that makes any day feel like a celebration.

INGREDIENTS

CHIMICHURRI

- 2 cups parsley leaves, finely chopped
- 3 garlic cloves, peeled and finely chopped
- 1 large shallot, peeled and finely chopped
- ½ cup extra virgin olive oil
- ⅓ cup red wine vinegar
- ¼ teaspoon sea salt, or more to taste (do not use iodized salt)
- ¼ teaspoon freshly ground black pepper, or more to taste

STEAMED CLAMS

- 6 pounds fresh clams, scrubbed
- ¼ cup sea salt
- 1 large lemon, cut into wedges

DIRECTIONS

For the chimichurri: Combine all the ingredients in a small bowl and set aside.

For the steamed clams: Place clean clams in a large bucket or bowl then add salt and enough water to cover the clams. Soak clams for 2 hours in the refrigerator.

After soaking, rinse the clams and place in a large pot with 2 cups of water. Bring water to a rapid boil over high heat. Reduce heat to medium. Cook the clams for about 7 minutes, or until the clams open. Discard any clams that do not open. Ladle clams into bowls with a slotted spoon.

Serve immediately with the chimichurri, and lemon wedges.

NUTRITION FACTS

Amount per serving | Calories 342 | Total Fat 27g | Saturated Fat 3.7g | Cholesterol 55mg | Sodium 602mg | Total Carbohydrate 5.1g | Dietary Fiber 1.5g | Total Sugars 0.7g | Protein 23.3g

THAI BEEF SALAD

Thai salads are so delicious because they feature a colorful array of vegetables and offer the perfect balance of savory, salty, sweet, bright, and tangy. This Thai Beef salad, known as Yum Nua, is loaded with aromatics like fresh herbs and shallots that make for a flavorful, gut-friendly meal.

PREP
10 MIN

COOK
25 MIN

SERVES
4

INGREDIENTS

DRESSING
- 1 clove garlic, peeled and finely chopped
- 2 tablespoons fresh cilantro
- 2 tablespoons plain rice vinegar
- 2 tablespoons lime juice
- 1 tablespoon coconut aminos
- 1 tablespoon fish sauce
- ¼ teaspoon stevia, or more to taste
- 2 teaspoons sesame oil
- 3 tablespoons avocado oil
- ¼ teaspoon kosher salt, or more to taste

SALAD
- 2 tablespoons avocado oil
- 1 New York strip steak, trimmed of excess fat (approx. 12 oz.)
- ¼ teaspoon kosher salt, or more to taste
- ¼ teaspoon freshly ground black pepper, or more to taste
- 6 cups mixed leaf lettuce, washed and torn
- 2 medium carrots, peeled and shredded
- 2 shallots, peeled and finely sliced
- 1 cup fresh mint leaves, chiffonade cut
- 1 cup fresh cilantro leaves, chopped

DIRECTIONS

For the dressing: Thoroughly whisk together all ingredients for the dressing in a small mixing bowl. Cover and chill until needed.

For the salad: Heat avocado oil in a large cast iron pan set over high heat until it just starts to smoke. As the pan pre-heats, season steak with salt and pepper on both sides.

When the pan is ready, carefully add seasoned steak. Leave undisturbed until a golden-brown crust forms underneath, 3 to 4 minutes. Flip and cook for a further 3 to 4 minutes until firm to the touch with a slight spring; a meat thermometer should register 135°F for medium-rare.

Remove steak from pan and rest under aluminum foil tent for at least 10 minutes.

While steak rests, divide lettuce, carrots, shallots, mint, and cilantro between 4 serving bowls.

Cut steak into thin strips and add to salad bowls, spooning the prepared dressing over the top of each before serving.

NUTRITION FACTS
*Amount per serving | Calories 406 |
Total Fat 25.5g | Saturated Fat 5.4g |
Cholesterol 73mg | Sodium 800mg |
Total Carbohydrate 13g | Dietary Fiber 3.1g |
Total Sugars 2.3g | Protein 31.4g*

DINNER

Much like lunch, your gut-friendly dinner template includes a foundation of cooked or raw vegetables, a side of protein, and healthy additions like fruits, fats, flours, resistant starches, and other things that accompany the Healthy Gut Zone diet. Many of the following recipes come together easily but are still delicious enough to serve with company. Spreading the flavors and colors of a healthy lifestyle to friends and family is easier than you think. (Tip: If you tend to experience acid reflux, try to eat smaller meals—especially at dinner. This will help reduce symptoms until you achieve the best long-term answer to acid reflux: getting your gut healthy again.)

FOUR-SPICE SALMON
WITH BOK CHOY

PREP
10 MIN

While good wild salmon needs little more than a bit of salt to shine, rubbing fresh salmon fillets with piquant spices takes dinner to a whole new flavor dimension. The blend of cumin, coriander, fennel, and fenugreek is popular in Ayurveda, India's traditional holistic medicine system. These spices are often steeped to make a digestion-boosting tea, so why not try cooking with them for a gut boost with dinner?

COOK
12 MIN

SERVES
4

INGREDIENTS

- 2 teaspoons cumin seeds
- 2 teaspoons coriander seeds
- 2 teaspoons fennel seeds
- 1 teaspoon fenugreek seeds
- 1 teaspoon kosher salt
- ½ teaspoon freshly ground black pepper
- 4 fresh wild salmon fillets, skinless and pin-boned, approx. 4 oz. each
- 2 tablespoons avocado oil, divided
- 2 bok choy, split in half
- 1 tablespoon fresh cilantro, finely chopped
- ½ teaspoon toasted sesame oil
- 1 lime, cut into wedges

DIRECTIONS

Place cumin, coriander, fennel, and fenugreek seeds in a small sauté pan over medium heat, stir and toast until aromatic, 2 to 3 minutes.

Tip the toasted seeds into a spice grinder or mortar and pestle and add the salt and pepper. Combine until coarsely ground. Rub spice mixture onto salmon fillets and brush with one of the tablespoons of avocado oil.

In a non-stick sauté or grill pan over medium-high heat, sear the salmon in the remaining tablespoon of avocado oil for about ten minutes. Flip the filets halfway through. Cook until firm to the touch and opaque in appearance.

While the salmon is cooking, steam bok choy in a covered steaming basket set over a saucepan of simmering water until tender, about 2 to 3 minutes.

Divide salmon between four plates, squeezing with fresh lime juice. Add steamed bok choy to the plates and drizzle with toasted sesame oil. Garnish with chopped cilantro and serve immediately.

NUTRITION FACTS

Amount per serving | Calories 376 | Total Fat 19.9g | Saturated Fat 2.6g | Cholesterol 78mg | Sodium 482mg | Total Carbohydrate 13.1g | Dietary Fiber 5.7g | Total Sugars 5.5g | Protein 41.8g

CARROT AND SWEET POTATO SOUP WITH COCONUT YOGURT, PEPITAS, AND BASIL

PREP
20 MIN

COOK
1 HR

SERVES
4

While the Healthy Gut Zone advises against excess starches, gut-healing carbs like sweet potatoes are a great addition to your meals in moderation. Sweet potatoes are a source of resistant starch—the carbohydrates that are not digested (they "resist" it) until they reach the large intestine, where they ferment and feed the good bacteria in the gut. Serving this soup cold boosts the resistant starch even more.

INGREDIENTS

- 3 tablespoons extra virgin olive oil
- ½ medium yellow onion, peeled and chopped
- 2 garlic cloves, peeled and finely chopped
- 1¼ teaspoons salt, divided, plus more to taste
- ½ teaspoon freshly ground black pepper, divided, plus more to taste
- 6 medium carrots, peeled and cut into 1-inch pieces
- 1 large sweet potato, peeled and cut into 1-inch cubes
- 2 teaspoons fresh ginger, peeled and grated
- 1 teaspoon ground cumin
- 6 cups organic free-range chicken bone broth
- ½ cup unsweetened coconut yogurt, for serving
- ¼ cup raw pepitas (pumpkin seeds), for serving
- 4 fresh basil leaves, for serving

DIRECTIONS

In a large saucepan or Dutch oven, heat oil over medium-low heat. Stir in the onion, garlic, ¼ teaspoon salt, and ¼ teaspoon pepper. Cook, stirring occasionally, until the onion is soft and translucent, 5 to 7 minutes.

Add carrots, sweet potato, ginger, cumin, and bone broth to the onion mixture. Bring to a boil over high heat, reduce heat to a simmer and cook until the vegetables are soft enough to blend, 25 to 30 minutes. Stir in remaining 1 teaspoon salt and ¼ teaspoon pepper.

Remove soup from heat and allow to cool for a few minutes. Remove the center cap of a blender lid. Fill the blender halfway with soup. Cover the hole in the lid with a paper towel to prevent splattering. Blend the soup until smooth and transfer to a serving bowl. Repeat the process with the remaining soup until it is all blended and smooth. Season to taste with more salt and pepper, if desired.

Ladle the soup into 4 bowls and top with a dollop of yogurt, pumpkin seeds, and basil leaves. Serve warm or cold.

NUTRITION FACTS
Amount per serving | Calories 248 |
Total Fat 12.1g | Saturated Fat 2.1g |
Cholesterol 0mg | Sodium 963mg |
Total Carbohydrate 21.5g | Dietary Fiber 4.8g |
Total Sugars 8.3g | Protein 16.2g

I like to serve these meatballs with carrot or sweet potato noodles to add fiber and an extra serving of gut-friendly vegetables. (You can easily make your own carrot noodles by baking long strips cut using a vegetable peeler!) Make sure your chicken is pastured, organic, or free-range—not soy or corn fed—to avoid excess lectins.

PREP
25 MIN

COOK
20 MIN

SERVES
6

INGREDIENTS

MEATBALLS

- 2 slices flaxseed bread, roughly torn into small pieces
- ¼ cup organic free-range chicken bone broth
- 1 pound organic free-range chicken (lean), ground
- 1 large organic free-range egg
- ½ cup fresh flat-leaf parsley, finely chopped
- ½ tablespoon fresh rosemary, finely chopped
- 1 teaspoon ground coriander
- 1 teaspoon ground cumin
- 1 tablespoon fresh lemon zest
- 1 tablespoon fresh lemon juice
- 1 ¼ teaspoons salt
- ½ teaspoon freshly ground black pepper
- 3 tablespoons extra virgin olive oil, plus more if needed

LEMON GARLIC SAUCE

- 2 tablespoons extra virgin olive oil
- 3 cloves garlic, peeled and minced
- ½ cup organic free-range chicken bone broth
- ½ teaspoon salt
- 2 tablespoons fresh lemon juice

DIRECTIONS

In a large bowl, combine flaxseed bread pieces and bone broth and let sit about 5 minutes while the broth softens the bread.

Add ground chicken, egg, parsley, rosemary, coriander, cumin, lemon zest, lemon juice, salt, and pepper to the bread mixture. Use hands or a large spoon to mix well.

Form the mixture into 1 ½-inch meatballs, 2 to 3 tablespoons each, and place on a baking sheet.

In a large cast iron or non-stick skillet, heat 3 tablespoons of olive oil over medium heat until shimmering. Add meatballs to the skillet, making sure not to crowd them, cooking in batches if needed. Use tongs to turn the meatballs every minute or so until they are browned on all sides, 6 to 8 minutes per batch, adding more oil if the skillet gets too dry. Transfer to a plate and set aside.

Drain any extra grease from the skillet and return the skillet to the stovetop.

Reheat the skillet over medium heat. Add olive oil and garlic. Use a large wooden spoon to scrape any of the brown bits from the pan while stirring the garlic, 1 to 2 minutes. Add bone broth to the skillet and turn the heat up to high. Bring the broth to a boil and continue to cook until reduced by half, 3 to 5 minutes. Stir in the salt and lemon juice and reduce the heat to medium.

Add meatballs back to the skillet with the sauce and continue to cook the meatballs until a thermometer inserted into the center of the meatballs registers 165°F. Serve immediately or refrigerate and serve within 2 days. To reheat meatballs, preheat oven to 350°F. Place the meatballs in a covered oven-safe dish and bake until warmed through, 10 to 12 minutes.

NUTRITION FACTS

Amount per serving | Calories 459 | Total Fat 15.4g | Saturated Fat 4g | Cholesterol 204mg | Sodium 714mg | Total Carbohydrate 4.4g | Dietary Fiber 1.8g | Total Sugars 0.7g | Protein 73g

LEMON GARLIC SHRIMP

PREP
15 MIN

COOK
5 MIN

SERVES
4

Here's a garlic pro-tip to maximize the allium's healthy antimicrobial benefits: Chop and/or mince your garlic ten to fifteen minutes before you need it, as this will release an enzyme called allicin that makes garlic's key healthy nutrients more digestible in your gut. Allicin has been linked to lower blood pressure, reduced cholesterol, and strengthened immune systems. Talk about a culinary hero!

INGREDIENTS

— 1 ¼ pounds raw shrimp (wild caught, medium, 41 to 50 count), peeled and deveined; tails intact

— ½ teaspoon salt

— ½ teaspoon freshly ground black pepper

— 2 tablespoons extra virgin olive oil

— 2 cloves garlic, peeled and minced

— 2 tablespoons water

— 2 tablespoons freshly squeezed lemon juice, plus 1 teaspoon

— 2 tablespoons fresh flat-leaf parsley, finely chopped

— Lemon wedges, for serving

DIRECTIONS

Season shrimp all over with salt and pepper.

In a large skillet, warm the oil over medium-high heat. Add the shrimp and garlic to the skillet and cook, stirring occasionally until the shrimp are pink and opaque, 3 to 5 minutes.

Turn off the heat and add 2 tablespoons water, the lemon juice, and chopped parsley. Stir shrimp to coat in the sauce. Serve immediately with lemon wedges, if desired.

NUTRITION FACTS

Amount per serving | Calories 205 | Total Fat 8.6g | Saturated Fat 1.4g | Cholesterol 276mg | Sodium 611mg | Total Carbohydrate 1.3g | Dietary Fiber 0.2g | Total Sugars 0.2g | Protein 29.9g

Sirloin steaks are a great lower-fat option, especially when you opt for grass-fed and grass-finished beef. Because they are on the leaner side of the steak spectrum, adding a flavorful pan sauce ensures every bite is tender and packed with flavor. Serve the steaks with a salad loaded with gut-friendly vegetables to add fiber and polyphenols to round out the meal.

PREP
20 MIN

COOK
20 MIN

SERVES
4

INGREDIENTS

- 4 sirloin steaks, grass-fed, approx. 6 oz. each
- 1 teaspoon salt, plus more to taste
- ½ teaspoon freshly ground black pepper, plus more to taste
- 4 tablespoons extra virgin olive oil, divided
- 1 cup organic beef stock
- 3 tablespoons arrowroot
- 1 medium yellow onion, peeled and thinly sliced
- 2 cloves garlic, peeled and finely chopped
- 1 pound fresh wild mushrooms, cleaned and sliced (i.e., oyster, shiitake, cremini, etc.)
- 1 tablespoon fresh sage, finely chopped
- ½ cup fresh flat-leaf parsley, chopped

DIRECTIONS

Let the steaks sit out at room temperature for 20 to 30 minutes before cooking. Pat steaks dry with paper towels and season all over with salt and pepper.

In a large cast iron or heavy bottomed skillet, heat 2 tablespoons of olive oil over medium-high heat until the pan is very hot, 2 to 3 minutes. Add the steak to the skillet and cook about 3 minutes per side for medium rare (125°F internal temperature), 6 minutes per side for medium (135°F internal temperature), or 9 minutes per side for well done (155°F internal temperature). Transfer the steaks to a cutting board to rest while making the pan sauce.

In a small bowl, stir together beef stock and arrowroot and set aside.

Reusing the unwashed skillet the steaks were cooked in, heat the skillet over medium heat. Add the remaining 2 tablespoons olive oil and the onion and cook, stirring occasionally, while scraping any browned bits left in the skillet, until the onions are softened, 3 to 6 minutes. Add the garlic and mushrooms to the skillet and cook, stirring occasionally until the mushrooms soften, about 3 minutes.

Add the stock mixture and sage to the skillet, bring to a boil, and cook until the pan sauce begins to thicken, 2 to 4 minutes. Stir in the parsley and season to taste with additional salt and pepper, if desired.

Slice the steaks across the grain, divide among 4 plates, and spoon the mushroom pan sauce over the steaks. Serve immediately.

NUTRITION FACTS

Amount per serving | Calories 407 | Total Fat 22.5g | Saturated Fat 5.1g | Cholesterol 114mg | Sodium 837mg | Total Carbohydrate 8.7g | Dietary Fiber 2.3g | Total Sugars 3.2g | Protein 43.5g

LOBSTER BASIL SALAD

PREP
10 MIN

SERVES
2

Most lobster salads are loaded with creamy sauces that drown out the delicate taste of the shellfish. This light, summery recipe uses fresh basil and simple seasonings, and begs to be enjoyed al fresco with a cold beverage and a warm breeze. Steaming a lobster yourself is an adventure that makes this treat more affordable, but feel free to purchase prepared lobster meat from a trustworthy seafood counter.

INGREDIENTS

- 2 tablespoons extra virgin olive oil
- 1 clove garlic, minced
- 3 tablespoons fresh lemon juice
- 2 tablespoons fresh basil, finely chopped
- ¼ teaspoon salt, or more to taste
- ¼ teaspoon freshly ground black pepper, or more to taste
- 4 cups mixed greens, washed
- 2 cups cooked lobster meat, tail, claw, knuckle (approx. 12 oz.)
- 1 fresh lemon, washed and sliced into wedges

DIRECTIONS

Whisk together olive oil, garlic, lemon juice, basil, salt, and pepper in a small bowl.

Divide the greens and lobster evenly among individual plates. Drizzle with dressing and season with additional salt and pepper, if desired. Garnish with lemon wedges.

NUTRITION FACTS

Amount per serving | Calories 286 | Total Fat 15.7g | Saturated Fat 2.5g | Cholesterol 212mg | Sodium 1007mg | Total Carbohydrate 8.4g | Dietary Fiber 2.1g | Total Sugars 2.7g | Protein 28.9g

STEAMED CLAMS IN GARLIC BROTH
WITH LEMON HERB CAULIFLOWER RICE

Clams are on my healing foods list for a good reason. They're a low-fat source of protein, they are one of the best dietary sources of Vitamin B12, and they're a good source of iron and selenium. Plus, they have the added benefit of making any meal feel like a celebration. I simply swap the typical accompanying baguette for flavorful cauliflower rice spiked with lemon, parsley, and basil to make this meal a gut-friendly home run.

PREP
15 MIN

COOK
25 MIN

SERVES
2

INGREDIENTS

- 1 small cauliflower head, washed and dried, leaves removed (approx. 10 oz.)

- 5 tablespoons extra virgin olive oil, divided

- ¼ cup fresh flat-leaf parsley, finely chopped, plus more for garnish

- ¼ cup fresh basil leaves, chopped, plus more leaves for garnish

- 1 tablespoon fresh lemon zest

- 2 tablespoons fresh lemon juice

- ¾ teaspoon salt

- ½ teaspoon freshly ground black pepper

- 1 shallot, peeled and finely chopped

- 3 cloves garlic, peeled and thinly sliced

- ½ cup wild fish broth

- 2 pounds wild littleneck clams, scrubbed clean

NUTRITION FACTS
Amount per serving | Calories 306 | Total Fat 22.8g | Saturated Fat 3.5g | Cholesterol 32mg | Sodium 1033mg | Total Carbohydrate 15.1g | Dietary Fiber 4.3g | Total Sugars 4g | Protein 13.8g

DIRECTIONS

Cut the cauliflower, including the core, into 2-inch pieces.

Place the cauliflower pieces in a food processor in batches. Pulse until it has the appearance of rice. Be careful not to over process it or it may become mushy. Set aside in a medium bowl.

In a large skillet, heat 3 tablespoons of olive oil over medium-high heat. Add the cauliflower and cook, stirring occasionally until heated through 5 to 8 minutes. Turn off the heat and stir in ¼ cup parsley, ¼ cup basil, lemon zest, lemon juice, salt, and pepper.

Meanwhile, in a large Dutch oven or saucepan, heat 2 remaining tablespoons of olive oil over medium heat. Add the shallot and cook until soft, 3 to 5 minutes. Stir in the garlic and cook until fragrant, about 1 minute.

Add fish broth and 1 cup of water and bring to a boil. Add clams, cover the pan, and cook until the clams open, 5 to 7 minutes. Discard any clams that have not opened.

To serve, divide the cauliflower rice between two large bowls and top each with half of the clams and a little of the clam broth. Sprinkle with more chopped parsley and basil leaves, if desired. Serve immediately.

PREP
15 MIN

COOK
20 MIN

SERVES
4

Eggs aren't only for breakfast! Good organic, free-range eggs have deeper colored yolks, which this recipe shows off like lustrous gold on every plate. Asparagus, delicious both cooked and raw, is an excellent source of two gut power tools: prebiotic fiber and polyphenols. If you can't find organic asparagus, don't fear. It's on the EWG's Clean Fifteen list of produce with the lowest amounts of pesticide residues.

INGREDIENTS

- 4 large eggs, organic free-range
- 1 pound asparagus, washed and tough ends trimmed
- 4 tablespoons extra virgin olive oil, divided
- 1 ¼ teaspoons salt, divided
- ¾ teaspoon freshly ground black pepper, divided
- 3 tablespoons shallot, peeled and finely chopped
- 2 tablespoons fresh lemon juice
- 2 teaspoons fresh tarragon, chopped
- 6 cups mixed baby greens

DIRECTIONS

Preheat the oven to 425°F with the rack in the middle. Have a bowl of ice water ready.

Fill a medium saucepan with 3 inches of water and bring to a boil over high heat. Reduce heat to medium. Use a large, slotted spoon to carefully lower the eggs into the water and boil the eggs for exactly 7 minutes. Immediately transfer the eggs to the bowl of ice water. Once cool, carefully peel the eggs and slice each egg in half. Set aside.

Meanwhile, arrange the asparagus in a single layer on a standard-sized baking pan. Drizzle with 1 tablespoon olive oil and sprinkle with ½ teaspoon salt and ¼ teaspoon pepper. Toss gently to coat. Roast in the oven until crisp-tender, 8 to 10 minutes.

In a large bowl, whisk together the remaining 3 tablespoons olive oil, shallot, lemon juice, tarragon, ¾ teaspoon salt, and ½ teaspoon pepper. Add the mixed baby greens, tossing gently to coat in the dressing. Divide the salad greens among 4 serving plates. Top with some of the asparagus and 2 egg halves. Serve immediately.

NUTRITION FACTS

Amount per serving | Calories 245 | Total Fat 19.3g | Saturated Fat 3.7g | Cholesterol 186mg | Sodium 903mg | Total Carbohydrate 10.8g | Dietary Fiber 3.8g | Total Sugars 2.6g | Protein 10.4g

PAN SEARED HALIBUT FILLETS

PREP
5 MIN

COOK
10 MIN

SERVES
4

Sometimes a dinner of simple seared fish is more satisfying than an elaborate meal. Pair this delicately seasoned halibut with any of the flavorful, gut-friendly, vegetable-packed salads in this book for a showstopper of a weeknight meal that will be ready in minutes. If you can't find halibut, this recipe also works with other low-mercury fish like wild flounder, wild tilapia, wild cod, and haddock.

INGREDIENTS

- 4 fresh halibut fillets, approx. 6 oz. each
- ½ teaspoon kosher salt
- ½ teaspoon freshly ground black pepper
- 1 tablespoon extra virgin olive oil
- 1 lime, washed and cut into wedges

DIRECTIONS

Season halibut fillets all over with salt and pepper.

Heat a large skillet over medium-high heat and add olive oil.

When hot, add the halibut and cook until opaque, 3 to 5 minutes per side, or until it has registered an internal temperature of 145°F. Serve immediately with lime wedges on the side.

NUTRITION FACTS

Amounts per serving | Calories 274 | Total Fat 8.6g | Saturated Fat 1.2g | Cholesterol 70mg | Sodium 408mg | Total Carbohydrate 1.9g | Dietary Fiber 0.5g | Total Sugars 0.3g | Protein 45.5g

This Asian-inspired soup infused with healing lemongrass, star anise, and ginger would make a refreshing, restorative dinner or starter for a gut-friendly dinner party. For a weeknight shortcut, feel free to use leftover chicken breasts or shrimp, which will cook faster. If you like noodles in your chicken soup, try adding some ribbons of carrot using a vegetable peeler.

INGREDIENTS

— 4 cups chicken broth

— 2 ribs celery, cleaned, trimmed, and thinly sliced

— 1 fresh ginger, 1" piece, peeled and thinly sliced

— 2 stalks lemongrass, crushed

— 1 star anise

— 1 pound boneless, skinless chicken breasts

— 2 limes, washed and cut into wedges

— ½ teaspoon salt, or more to taste

— ½ teaspoon freshly ground black pepper, or more to taste

— 1 bunch Thai basil, leaves only

DIRECTIONS

In a large pan over medium-high heat, bring chicken broth to a boil. Add the celery, ginger, lemongrass, and star anise and simmer for 10 minutes.

Using a sharp knife, cut the chicken into thin strips. Add the chicken to the pot and cook for about 5 minutes, or until the chicken cooks through.

Remove the lemongrass and star anise and add the lime wedges. Season the soup to taste, if desired, with salt and freshly ground black pepper. Ladle into 4 bowls and garnish with Thai basil leaves.

NUTRITION FACTS

Amount per serving | Calories 318 | Total Fat 7.2g | Saturated Fat 0.4g | Cholesterol 143mg | Sodium 1186mg | Total Carbohydrate 7.4g | Dietary Fiber 1.6g | Total Sugars 1.7g | Protein 53.1g

GRILLED SHRIMP WITH JICAMA SALAD

Native to Mexico, jicama is a low carb, gut-friendly vegetable with a delightfully juicy and fresh crunch, similar to an Asian pear or a water chestnut. It's a great, low-carb source of insoluble fiber and prebiotic resistant starch, which makes it a good choice for pretty much any meal! In this recipe, it's mixed into a fresh herb salad to offer a cooling counterpoint to grilled shrimp.

PREP
15 MIN

COOK
10 MIN

SERVES
4

INGREDIENTS

- 2 medium jicamas, peeled and julienned
- 1 tablespoon fresh chives, finely chopped
- ½ tablespoon fresh tarragon, finely chopped
- 3 ½ tablespoons fresh lime juice
- 4 tablespoons extra virgin olive oil, divided
- 3 tablespoons kefir, plain unsweetened
- ½ teaspoon kosher salt, divided
- ½ teaspoon freshly ground black pepper, divided
- 1 ½ pounds large raw shrimp, peeled, deveined, and tails removed
- 2 radishes, washed and thinly sliced

DIRECTIONS

In a large mixing bowl, combine jicama, chives, tarragon, lime juice, half of the olive oil, and kefir. Season with half of the salt and pepper and toss until everything is well incorporated. Set aside.

Preheat the grill or sauté pan to high.

In another large bowl, add shrimp, the remaining olive oil, salt, and pepper and toss together well. Cook the shrimp for 2 to 3 minutes per side, or until no longer opaque, and remove from grill pan.

Divide the jicama salad between individual plates. Add equal portions of the shrimp to salad plates, garnish with the radish slices, and serve immediately.

NUTRITION FACTS

Amount per serving | Calories 381 | Total Fat 16.3g | Saturated Fat 2.7g | Cholesterol 224mg | Sodium 317mg | Total Carbohydrate 32g | Dietary Fiber 16.5g | Total Sugars 6.5g | Protein 27.4g

73

SEARED TUNA STEAKS
WITH LEMON AND PARSLEY SAUCE

PREP
10 MIN

MARINATE
30 MIN

COOK
10 MIN

It's amazing how much flavor a fresh herb sauce can bring to a simple dish. This warm lemon parsley drizzle would be equally delicious over chicken breasts or shrimp. When shopping for tuna steaks, look for skipjack tuna for a lower-mercury option.

SERVES
4

INGREDIENTS

— 2 tuna steaks, approx. 8 oz. each

— ¾ cup extra virgin olive oil, divided

— 2 lemons, zested and juiced

— ½ teaspoon salt, divided

— ½ teaspoon freshly ground black pepper, divided

— ½ cup flat-leaf parsley, chopped

— ¼ white onion, peeled and finely chopped

— 1 large shallot, peeled and finely chopped

— 1 clove garlic, peeled and finely chopped

— 1 tablespoon avocado oil

— 1 lemon, thinly sliced

DIRECTIONS

Trim any remaining skin or dark spots from the tuna. Rinse under cold running water and pat dry with paper towels. Brush the tuna steaks with ¼ cup olive oil and 1 ½ tablespoons lemon juice, season generously with half the salt and pepper. Place in a container, cover with plastic wrap, and marinate in the refrigerator for at least 30 minutes, turning once or twice.

In a skillet over low heat, combine ½ cup olive oil, parsley, onion, shallot, garlic, two tablespoons of lemon juice, lemon zest, and remaining salt and pepper. Simmer gently, stirring to incorporate, for about 4 minutes. Remove from heat and set aside.

Bring a frying pan, cast iron pan, or grill pan to high heat with avocado oil. Once hot, add the tuna steaks to the pan and sear for 4 to 5 minutes per side (for medium) or until preferred doneness is reached. Do not overcook.

Remove tuna from the pan. Spoon sauce over the top of the tuna steaks. Add additional salt and pepper to taste, if needed. Serve the dish immediately with sliced lemon.

NUTRITION FACTS

Amount per serving | Calories 395 | Total Fat 18.3g | Saturated Fat 2.7g | Cholesterol 96mg | Sodium 376mg | Total Carbohydrate 7.1g | Dietary Fiber 1.7g | Total Sugars 1.4g | Protein 50.8g

Inspired by the classic Italian-American dish, Chicken Marsala, this comforting dinner is perfect for sharing with friends and family. Feel free to substitute any fresh mushrooms here—thinly sliced portobello, shiitake, oyster, porcinis, or a mix of wild mushrooms would be equally delicious. I'd serve this alongside some mashed cauliflower for a true comfort food feast.

PREP
20 MIN

COOK
1 HR 5 MIN

SERVES
4

INGREDIENTS

- 2 tablespoons avocado oil
- 8 bone-in, skin-on chicken thighs
- ½ teaspoon kosher salt, or more to taste
- ¼ teaspoon freshly ground black pepper, or more to taste
- 4 cups button mushrooms, washed and sliced
- ½ medium onion, peeled and finely diced
- 2 medium carrots, peeled, trimmed, finely chopped
- 2 cloves garlic, peeled and minced
- 2 fresh bay leaves
- 1 cup dry marsala wine
- 1 ½ cups chicken bone broth or stock
- 4 tablespoons unsweetened almond milk
- 4 fresh thyme sprigs

DIRECTIONS

Heat avocado oil in a large skillet or a Dutch oven with a tight-fitting lid over medium-high heat. Pat the chicken pieces dry and season with salt and pepper. To avoid crowding the pan, brown ½ the chicken at a time, skin-side down, for 5 minutes, then turn the chicken and brown 3 minutes more. Remove the chicken from the pan and set aside.

Add the mushrooms to the hot pan, browning the mushrooms for 10 to 15 minutes. Add the onion, carrot, garlic, and bay leaves. Stir for 10 minutes more to soften.

Add the marsala and chicken broth, scraping up the brown bits from the bottom of the pan. Slowly incorporate the almond milk. Add the chicken back to the pot and arrange the vegetables and mushrooms on top. Cover and braise at a low simmer for 30 minutes over low heat. Remove bay leaves and garnish with thyme before serving.

NUTRITION FACTS

Amount per serving | Calories 367 | Total Fat 19g | Saturated Fat 4.6g | Cholesterol 86mg | Sodium 695mg | Total Carbohydrate 10g | Dietary Fiber 2.3g | Total Sugars 4g | Protein 28.1g

PREP
10 MIN

COOK
20 MIN

SERVES
4

This soup is a gut-friendly green machine! The cashews and coconut milk make it deliciously creamy without dairy. (Be sure to use the underappreciated broccoli stems, which contain the most fiber, and the leaves, which are rich in antioxidants and vitamins E and K.)

INGREDIENTS

- 2 tablespoons avocado oil
- 1 large broccoli head, washed and cut into 1-inch pieces (approx. 6 cups)
- 2 tablespoons raw cashews
- 1 tablespoon light coconut milk
- 1 small white onion, peeled and diced
- 2 cloves garlic, peeled and minced
- ½ teaspoon kosher salt, or more to taste
- ¼ teaspoon freshly ground black pepper, or more to taste
- 4 cups chicken broth
- 4 cups baby spinach, washed
- 3 tablespoons fresh parsley leaves, finely chopped

DIRECTIONS

Heat avocado oil in a Dutch oven set over medium heat. Add broccoli, cashews, coconut milk, onion, garlic, salt, and pepper. Sweat the broccoli until softened, stirring occasionally, about 6 to 8 minutes.

Stir in chicken broth. Add baby spinach. Simmer for a further 5 minutes, stirring from time to time.

Remove from heat and purée soup with an immersion blender or in batches using a food processor or blender. Once blended, cover and keep warm over low heat for another five minutes.

Ladle soup into warm bowls and garnish with parsley leaves. Serve immediately.

NUTRITION FACTS

Amount per serving | Calories 167 | Total Fat 8.4g | Saturated Fat 2g | Cholesterol 0mg | Sodium 1126mg | Total Carbohydrate 15.1g | Dietary Fiber 5g | Total Sugars 4.3g | Protein 10.7g

CHICKEN AND VEGETABLE SOUP

This is the chicken soup you'll want to reach for whenever you're feeling under the weather. The comforting flavors of celery, carrot, and bay leaves will remind you of the chicken soup of your childhood, while the kohlrabi adds some gut-healing fiber to get you back to your best. Roasting the chicken makes for the richest broth!

PREP
15 MIN

COOK
1 HR

SERVES
4

INGREDIENTS

- 1 medium whole chicken, cleaned, gutted, and jointed (or substitute with various bone-in pieces)
- 2 tablespoons extra virgin olive oil
- 1 teaspoon kosher salt
- 1 teaspoon freshly ground black pepper
- 6 celery stalks, peeled and cut into batons
- 2 kohlrabi, peeled and cut into batons
- 1 large carrot, peeled and cut into batons
- 2 bay leaves
- 6 cups water

DIRECTIONS

Preheat oven to 425°F.

Rub chicken pieces with olive oil and season with salt and pepper. Place on a roasting rack set inside a roasting pan.

Roast until skin is golden-brown, about 30 to 40 minutes.

In the meantime, combine vegetables, bay leaves, and water in a large pot. Bring to a boil and then reduce heat to a gentle simmer.

Remove chicken from oven when ready and transfer to the pot along with any accumulated juices, stirring well.

Simmer until chicken is cooked through, about 15 to 20 minutes.

When ready, remove chicken pieces from broth and pull apart, discarding the bones. Divide meat among soup bowls and top with broth. Remove bay leaves before serving.

NUTRITION FACTS
Amount per serving | Calories 335 | Total Fat 12.8g | Saturated Fat 2.5g | Cholesterol 97mg | Sodium 734mg | Total Carbohydrate 12.5g | Dietary Fiber 5.9g | Total Sugars 4.8g | Protein 42.7g

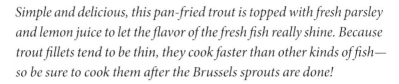

PREP
15 MIN

COOK
50 MIN

SERVES
4

Simple and delicious, this pan-fried trout is topped with fresh parsley and lemon juice to let the flavor of the fresh fish really shine. Because trout fillets tend to be thin, they cook faster than other kinds of fish— so be sure to cook them after the Brussels sprouts are done!

INGREDIENTS

BRUSSELS SPROUTS

- 1 ¼ pounds Brussels sprouts, cleaned and halved
- 3 tablespoons extra virgin olive oil
- 1 tablespoon white balsamic vinegar
- ½ teaspoon kosher salt, or more to taste
- ¼ teaspoon freshly ground black pepper, or more to taste

TROUT

- 4 tablespoons extra virgin olive oil
- 8 fresh trout fillets, skin-on
- ½ teaspoon kosher salt, or more to taste
- ¼ teaspoon freshly ground black pepper, or more to taste
- 1 tablespoon fresh parsley, finely chopped
- 1 lemon, cut into wedges, for serving

DIRECTIONS

For the Brussels sprouts: Preheat the oven to 350°F.

Toss together the Brussels sprouts, olive oil, balsamic vinegar, and salt and pepper on a large roasting tray.

Roast in the oven for 40 to 45 minutes until the sprouts are tender and browned, turning a few times during cooking.

Remove from the oven and transfer to a serving platter. Set aside and keep warm until fish is done.

For the trout: Heat the oil in a large skillet over medium-high heat. Season the trout with salt and pepper.

Add the trout to the hot skillet, skin side down, and sear for about 3 minutes. Carefully turn the fish over and cook for an additional 3 minutes, or until the fish registers a temperature of 145°F.

Transfer to a serving platter and garnish with parsley and lemons. Serve immediately together with the Brussels sprouts.

NUTRITION FACTS

Amount per serving | Calories 423 | Total Fat 25g | Saturated Fat 4g | Cholesterol 92mg | Sodium 701mg | Total Carbohydrate 14.5g | Dietary Fiber 5.8g | Total Sugars 3.5g | Protein 38.1g

These asparagus-beef rollups are great for a quick dinner as well as an appetizer for a gut-friendly dinner party. The miso-mustard mixture truly elevates it into a shareable delight! Make a double batch and have a satisfying lunch the following day.

PREP
15 MIN

COOK
20 MIN

SERVES
4

INGREDIENTS

- 8 thick asparagus spears, washed, peeled, with woody ends removed
- ½ teaspoon kosher salt
- ½ teaspoon freshly ground black pepper
- 1 teaspoon white miso
- 1 tablespoon Dijon mustard
- 8 thin slices roast beef, cold
- 2 tablespoons extra virgin olive oil
- 2 scallions, washed and chopped

DIRECTIONS

Preheat oven to 325°F.

Bring a large saucepan of salted water to a boil. Blanch the asparagus spears in the boiling water for 2 to 3 minutes or until tender.

Drain and refresh immediately in a large bowl of ice water. Remove from the ice water after 3 minutes and pat dry. Season with salt and pepper.

In a small bowl, combine miso with ¼ cup water and Dijon mustard.

Spread the slices of roast beef with a thin layer of the miso-mustard mixture. Place an asparagus spear at one end of the slice and roll into a cigar shape, enveloping the asparagus in the center.

Place the prepared spears on a sheet pan and drizzle with olive oil. Heat them in the oven for 7 to 10 minutes, or until warm.

Arrange on a platter and sprinkle with chopped scallion before serving.

NUTRITION FACTS

Amount per serving | Calories 285 | Total Fat 14.4g | Saturated Fat 5g | Cholesterol 75mg | Sodium 2304mg | Total Carbohydrate 9.3g | Dietary Fiber 2g | Total Sugars 2g | Protein 28.1g

PREP
15 MIN

MARINATE
1 HR

COOK
10 MIN

SERVES
4

The Thai-inspired marinade is the star of this dish—that super fresh flavor combo of lemongrass, fish sauce, and slightly sweet coconut aminos is a real winner. I also like to add button mushrooms to these skewers and serve them alongside a crunchy cabbage salad for a summery meal.

INGREDIENTS

- 1 shallot, peeled and chopped
- ¼ teaspoon kosher salt
- ½ teaspoon freshly ground black pepper
- 1 teaspoon fish sauce
- 1 tablespoon coconut aminos
- 1 tablespoon sesame oil
- 1 stalk lemongrass, trimmed and minced
- 1 tablespoon extra virgin olive oil
- 1 pound tri-tip steak, well-trimmed
- 1 large red onion, peeled and cut into 1-inch chunks
- 16 metal skewers
- 1 cup fresh cilantro

DIRECTIONS

In a small bowl, combine the shallot, salt, pepper, fish sauce, coconut aminos, sesame oil, and lemongrass. Set aside.

Slice the beef across the grain into thin strips, about ¼ inch thick, 1 inch wide, and 2 to 3 inches long. Add the meat to the marinade and combine. Cover with plastic wrap and marinate at room temperature for 1 hour.

To grill the beef, preheat a gas grill to medium-high or heat a grill pan on high and add olive oil. Meanwhile, skewer 1 to 2 pieces of meat onto each kabob alternating with slices of red onion. Grill the skewers for 3 to 4 minutes on each side or until the beef is nicely browned. Sprinkle with fresh cilantro leaves to garnish.

NUTRITION FACTS

Amount per serving | Calories 368 | Total Fat 21.9g | Saturated Fat 6.5g | Cholesterol 76mg | Sodium 356mg | Total Carbohydrate 5.5g | Dietary Fiber 0.8g | Total Sugars 1.3g | Protein 35.5g

Baby kale is a fantastic green for gut-friendly salads. While mature kale can be on the tougher side, delicate baby kale is a great "gateway green" for folks who tend to stick with lettuce and spinach. I recommend opting for organic kale to avoid excess pesticides.

PREP
15 MIN

MARINATE
30 MIN

COOK
20 MIN

SERVES
4

INGREDIENTS

GRILLED CHICKEN

— ½ cup lemon juice

— 3 tablespoons extra virgin olive oil, divided

— 1 clove garlic, peeled and minced

— ½ teaspoon onion powder

— ¼ teaspoon kosher salt

— ¼ teaspoon freshly ground black pepper

— 4 boneless, skinless, organic free-range chicken breasts

— 1 medium onion, peeled and cut into wedges

WILTED BABY KALE

— 2 tablespoons extra virgin olive oil

— 2 cloves garlic, peeled and minced

— 1 large head baby kale, washed thoroughly and dried

— ¼ teaspoon kosher salt

— ¼ teaspoon freshly ground black pepper

— 2 tablespoons balsamic vinegar (optional)

DIRECTIONS

For grilled chicken: Combine lemon juice, 2 tablespoons olive oil, garlic, onion powder, salt, and pepper in a large re-sealable plastic storage bag. Secure the seal and shake the mixture to blend. Place the chicken in the bag and squeeze the bag to coat the chicken thoroughly. Marinate in the refrigerator for at least 30 minutes, turning occasionally. Remove chicken and discard the marinade.

Heat grill pan or non-stick frying pan over medium-high heat with remaining tablespoon of olive oil. Place chicken on prepared pan and cook 6 to 8 minutes per side or until chicken is no longer pink in the middle and juices run clear. Set aside.

For wilted baby kale: Heat the olive oil in a large skillet over medium-high heat. Add the garlic, stirring with a wooden spoon to avoid burning. Add the kale and move it around the skillet using tongs. Season with salt and pepper and continue cooking until slightly wilted but still crisp, about 3 to 4 minutes.

Divide the wilted kale among 4 plates. Drizzle with balsamic vinegar and top with the grilled chicken breast. Serve immediately.

NUTRITION FACTS

Amount per serving | Calories 303 | Total Fat 12.6g | Saturated Fat 2.9g | Cholesterol 98mg | Sodium 437mg | Total Carbohydrate 8.6g | Dietary Fiber 1.8g | Total Sugars 0.8g | Protein 41.7g

LETTUCE WRAPPED VEGGIE BURGERS
WITH TANGY SAUCE

This recipe requires a bit more prep work than most of my go-to meals, but the results are worth the effort. Unlike some "veggie" burgers that are packed with beans or soy, these patties are powered by vegetables like carrots, cauliflower, spinach, and sweet potato.

INGREDIENTS

PICKLED RED ONIONS

- 1 large red onion, peeled and thinly sliced
- ⅓ cup apple cider vinegar
- ⅓ cup red wine vinegar
- ¼ teaspoon kosher salt, or more to taste

TANGY BURGER SAUCE

- ¼ cup kefir
- ½ cup unsweetened coconut yogurt
- ¼ cup carrots, peeled and shredded
- 2 teaspoons apple cider vinegar
- 3 teaspoons avocado oil
- 1 teaspoon white miso
- ¼ teaspoon kosher salt, or more to taste
- ¼ teaspoon white pepper, to taste
- 1 tablespoon fresh chives, finely chopped
- 2 teaspoons fresh mint leaves, finely chopped

VEGGIE PATTIES

- 4 tablespoons avocado oil, divided
- ½ small yellow onion, peeled and finely chopped
- 1 clove garlic, peeled and minced

- 1 teaspoon dried basil
- ½ teaspoon dried oregano
- ½ teaspoon coriander
- ½ teaspoon kosher salt
- ½ teaspoon freshly ground black pepper
- ½ cup carrots, peeled and shredded
- 1 cup spinach leaves, cleaned, steamed, and finely chopped
- ½ cup cauliflower, steamed, and finely chopped
- 1 sweet potato, steamed, skin removed, and mashed
- 3 cups millet, cooked
- 1 teaspoon ground flax
- 1 large egg, beaten
- 1 tablespoon arrowroot powder, plus extra for dusting

TO ASSEMBLE

- 8 large lettuce leaves
- 1 large avocado, halved, peeled, pitted, and thinly sliced

PREP
1 HR

MARINATE
20 MIN

CHILL
30 MIN

DIRECTIONS

For the pickled red onions: In a small bowl, combine all the ingredients. Let marinate for about 20 minutes. Drain from the vinegar and set aside.

For the tangy burger sauce: Combine all ingredients except the chives and mint in a blender (or a small bowl for a chunkier sauce). Once smooth, pour the sauce into a small bowl, add the chives and mint, and set aside.

For the patties: Heat 2 tablespoons avocado oil in a large sauté pan set over medium heat. Add the onion, garlic, basil, oregano, coriander, salt, and pepper.

COOK
10 MIN

Sauté for 5 to 6 minutes, until softened. Add the carrots, spinach, cauliflower, sweet potato, and millet and cook for a further 2 to 3 minutes. Remove from the pan and place cooked vegetables in a large bowl.

Add the flax, egg, and arrowroot to the bowl, mashing well until combined. Shape mixture into four large patties and chill on a lined baking sheet in the refrigerator for 30 minutes.

SERVES
4

After chilling, dust the patties with a little extra arrowroot powder, shaking off the excess.

Heat remaining avocado oil in a large sauté pan set over moderate heat until hot. Pan-fry the patties for 4 to 5 minutes per side, until golden-brown on the outside. Remove from the pan and set aside to cool.

To assemble: Line four lettuce leaves with slices of avocado. Set the patties on the avocado slices and spread with the sauce. Serve topped with the remaining lettuce leaves.

NUTRITION FACTS

Amount per serving | Calories 347 | Total Fat 12.8g | Saturated Fat 2.9g |
Cholesterol 49mg | Sodium 126mg | Total Carbohydrate 48g | Dietary Fiber 9g |
Total Sugars 6.7g | Protein 11.4g

PREP
10 MIN

COOK
1 HR

SERVES
4

Sometimes simple is best. This one-pan meal is quick to prepare and throw in the oven while you get on with your evening. Make a double batch and enjoy savory chicken slices over salad for lunch the next day.

INGREDIENTS

- 4 tablespoons extra virgin olive oil, plus extra for greasing
- 4 garlic cloves, peeled and finely sliced
- 1 pound fresh carrots, peeled and trimmed
- 4 boneless, skinless, organic free-range chicken breasts
- ½ teaspoon kosher salt
- ¼ teaspoon freshly ground black pepper
- 1 lemon, juiced
- ½ cup fresh parsley, chopped
- 2 tablespoons fresh thyme, chopped

DIRECTIONS

Preheat oven to 375°F. Grease a large baking dish with a small amount of olive oil.

Sprinkle garlic on the bottom of the dish and add carrots in a single layer. Arrange chicken breasts on top of and in between carrots.

Season with salt and pepper. Drizzle with 4 tablespoons olive oil, lemon juice, and chopped herbs.

Bake for about 20 minutes. Turn chicken pieces over and spoon juices over chicken and carrots.

Reduce oven to 325°F. Roast for 15 to 25 minutes more or until the chicken is browned and cooked through. The thickest part of the breasts should register at least 165°F on a meat thermometer.

Remove from oven and let stand briefly before serving.

NUTRITION FACTS

Amount per serving | Calories 322 | Total Fat 8.2g | Saturated Fat 1.1g | Cholesterol 140mg | Sodium 595mg | Total Carbohydrate 14.9g | Dietary Fiber 4g | Total Sugars 6.1g | Protein 45.6g

RIBEYE STEAK WITH PORCINI MUSHROOM SALT AND SALSA VERDE

PREP
40 MIN

COOK
35 MIN

SERVES
4

When grilling steaks, keep the "less is more" rule in mind. That means less seasoning (only salt and pepper is needed), less turning (only once), and no punctures with a fork (use tongs) to maximize flavor and tenderness. This recipe finishes off a simply grilled steak with flavorful mushrooms and zesty salsa verde.

INGREDIENTS

- 1 tablespoon avocado oil
- 1 bone-in ribeye steak, trimmed of fat (approx. 2 pounds)
- ½ teaspoon kosher salt
- ¼ teaspoon freshly ground black pepper
- 1 oz. dried porcini mushrooms
- 1 teaspoon salt
- ½ cup extra virgin olive oil, divided
- 2 tablespoons baby capers, in brine, drained
- 2 cloves garlic, peeled and chopped
- 1 teaspoon lemon zest
- 1 cup fresh flat-leaf parsley

DIRECTIONS

Allow steak to stand at room temperature for at least 30 minutes prior to cooking.

Brush a stovetop grill pan or skillet with avocado oil. Preheat pan over high heat. Season the steak with salt and pepper on all sides.

Cook the steak until charred all over and slightly springy to the touch, turning once, about 6 to 8 minutes per side. When ready, the thickest part should reach at least 135°F on a meat thermometer.

Meanwhile, pulse porcini mushrooms with 1 teaspoon salt in a food processor until finely chopped. Transfer to a small bowl.

In same food processor bowl, combine ¼ cup olive oil with capers, garlic, lemon zest, and parsley. Pulse until finely chopped.

Transfer the salsa to a serving bowl and stir in the remaining ¼ cup olive oil.

When ready to serve, slice steak and garnish with prepared salsa verde and porcini mushroom salt.

NUTRITION FACTS
Amount per serving | Calories 446 | Total Fat 48.3g | Saturated Fat 15.2g | Cholesterol 80mg | Sodium 1073mg | Total Carbohydrate 5.6g | Dietary Fiber 2.6g | Total Sugars 0.3g | Protein 20.4g

PREP
20 MIN

MARINATE
20 MIN

These chicken legs provide a tropical spin on roasted chicken and have the snackable quality of bar food, only with better-for-you, gut-healing ingredients. Green mangoes are a great source of resistant starches that feed the good bacteria in your gut and are much lower in sugar than ripe mangoes. Think of them more like vegetables than fruit and add them to salads and other savory dishes.

COOK
50 MIN

SERVES
4

INGREDIENTS

GREEN MANGO SALSA

- 2 green mangoes, peeled and diced
- 3 tablespoons fresh cilantro, finely chopped
- 1 small red onion, peeled and finely chopped
- 2 teaspoons fresh lime juice
- ¼ teaspoon ground coriander
- ¼ teaspoon sea salt, or more to taste
- ¼ teaspoon freshly ground black pepper, or more to taste

CHICKEN LEGS

- 2 tablespoons fish sauce
- 2 tablespoons avocado oil
- 2 tablespoons coconut aminos
- ¼ cup fresh cilantro, finely chopped
- 1 garlic clove, peeled and minced
- 1 teaspoon fresh ginger, peeled and minced
- 1 tablespoon sesame seeds
- 6 whole skinless chicken legs
- ¼ cup fresh cilantro leaves

DIRECTIONS

For the salsa: In a medium bowl, combine all ingredients and gently mix. Cover and refrigerate until ready to use.

For the chicken: In a baking dish, combine fish sauce, avocado oil, coconut aminos, chopped cilantro, garlic, ginger, and sesame seeds. Add chicken and toss to coat with the marinade. Marinate for at least 20 minutes in the refrigerator.

Preheat oven to 400ºF.

Transfer the chicken to a baking sheet and roast for 45 to 50 minutes, or until cooked through. Serve with mango salsa and garnish with fresh cilantro.

NUTRITION FACTS

*Amount per serving | Calories 399 |
Total Fat 12.7g | Saturated Fat 3.4g |
Cholesterol 134mg | Sodium 869mg |
Total Carbohydrate 30.4g | Dietary Fiber 3.5g |
Total Sugars 24.5g | Protein 40.8g*

These fish cakes are a fun spin on crab cakes or fish burgers. Serve them with a colorful cauliflower-carrot hash for a totally satisfying low carb dinner that will keep your gut happy. Serve the leftovers with leafy greens for a stellar weekday lunch.

PREP
15 MIN

COOK
25 MIN

SERVES
4

INGREDIENTS

CAULIFLOWER-CARROT HASH
- 1 tablespoon avocado oil
- 2 shallots, peeled and finely chopped
- 2 medium carrots, washed, peeled, and shredded
- 1 ½ cups cauliflower rice, prepared
- ¼ teaspoon white pepper
- ¼ teaspoon nutmeg
- ½ teaspoon salt, or more to taste
- ¼ teaspoon freshly ground black pepper, or more to taste

SALMON CAKES
- 1 pound fresh salmon, cooked
- 1 clove garlic, peeled and finely chopped
- 3 tablespoons fresh chives, finely chopped
- 2 tablespoons fresh parsley, finely chopped
- 1 teaspoon dried basil leaves
- ¼ cup almond flour
- 2 teaspoons Dijon mustard
- 2 large eggs, beaten
- ½ teaspoon salt, or more to taste
- ¼ teaspoon freshly ground black pepper, or more to taste
- 1 tablespoon avocado oil

DIRECTIONS

For the cauliflower-carrot hash: Add avocado oil to a large skillet set over medium-high heat. Sauté shallots until soft and translucent, about 3 minutes. Add the remaining hash ingredients to the pan. Cook until softened and vegetables begin to lightly brown. Remove from heat and set aside.

For the salmon cakes: Combine all the ingredients except avocado oil in a medium bowl. Form the mixture into four patties.

Heat a large skillet over medium-high heat with avocado oil. Cook the cakes for 2 to 3 minutes on each side or until golden brown.

Divide the salmon cakes between four plates and serve alongside hash. Best served warm.

NUTRITION FACTS
*Amount per serving | Calories 336 |
Total Fat 17.6g | Saturated Fat 2.8g |
Cholesterol 168mg | Sodium 755mg |
Total Carbohydrate 8.1g | Dietary Fiber 2.2g |
Total Sugars 2.8g | Protein 38.1g*

PREP
10 MIN

COOK
20 MIN

SERVES
6

This recipe would make an excellent appetizer for a gut-friendly dinner party. Slow cooking the leeks brings out their natural sweetness, and the drizzle of balsamic pushes that sweetness even farther. (Tip: Watch the scallops carefully so they don't overcook.)

INGREDIENTS

BALSAMIC REDUCTION
— 1 cup good quality balsamic vinegar

LEEKS
— 3 leeks, thinly sliced into discs, then cleaned
— 1 tablespoon olive oil
— Kosher salt, to taste
— freshly ground black pepper, to taste

SCALLOPS
— 2 pounds sea scallops, tough tendon removed
— ¼ cup avocado oil
— 3 tablespoons fresh thyme, finely chopped
— 2 cloves of garlic, finely chopped
— Kosher salt, to taste
— freshly ground black pepper, to taste

DIRECTIONS

For the balsamic reduction: In a small saucepan, reduce the balsamic vinegar over a low boil until the liquid coats the back of a metal spoon when inserted into the pot. Set aside.

For the leeks: Add the leek and olive oil to a pan and sauté until tender, about 7 to 8 minutes. Season with salt and pepper. Set aside.

For the scallops: In a saucepan over medium heat, heat the avocado oil. Add the thyme and garlic. Cook until fragrant but not brown, about 1 to 2 minutes.

In the meantime, rinse the scallops under cold running water, drain well, and pat dry with paper towels.

Brush the scallops with about ½ of the oil mixture. Season with salt and pepper. Place scallops in a fry or grill pan set over high heat. Cook for about 2 to 3 minutes on one side and flip to cook for about 1 minute on the following side. Do not overcook.

Serve immediately over the leeks and drizzle with the balsamic reduction and remaining oil mixture.

NUTRITION FACTS
Amount per serving | Calories 207 | Total Fat 4.9g | Saturated Fat 0.8g | Cholesterol 50mg | Sodium 449mg | Total Carbohydrate 12.1g | Dietary Fiber 1.8g | Total Sugars 2g | Protein 26.4g

This curried seafood soup is packed with Thai aromatics—like lemongrass, garlic, ginger, and curry spices—taking shellfish to gourmet territory. For ingredients you don't always stock, such as coconut aminos, fish sauce, and lemongrass paste, look in the Asian section of your grocery store. Pair the comforting one-pot soup with a fresh salad for a complete meal.

PREP
20 MIN

COOK
50 MIN

SERVES
4

INGREDIENTS

- 3 teaspoons avocado oil
- ½ teaspoon fresh ginger, peeled and finely chopped
- 2 cloves garlic, peeled and finely chopped
- 1 shallot, peeled and finely chopped
- 1 teaspoon curry powder
- 1 teaspoon lemongrass paste
- 1⅔ cups low fat coconut milk
- 5 cups seafood broth
- 1 lime, juiced
- 2 teaspoons coconut aminos
- 2 teaspoons fish sauce
- ½ teaspoon kosher salt, or more to taste
- ½ teaspoon freshly ground black pepper, or more to taste
- 12 oz. fresh jumbo shrimp, peeled and deveined (approx. 2 cups)
- 12 oz. fresh squid rings (approx. 2 cups)
- ½ cup fresh cilantro leaves
- 1 lime, sliced into wedges, for serving

DIRECTIONS

Heat a large pot or Dutch oven with avocado oil over medium heat. Add ginger, garlic, shallot, curry powder, and lemongrass paste and sauté for 2 to 3 minutes.

Add the coconut milk and seafood broth and bring the soup to a low simmer for 40 minutes.

Then, incorporate the lime juice, coconut aminos, and fish sauce. Season with salt and pepper.

Add the seafood and cook for another 2 to 4 minutes or until the seafood is fully cooked and the shrimp and squid are opaque.

Stir in the cilantro leaves and then ladle into serving bowls. Serve immediately with fresh lime wedges.

NUTRITION FACTS

Amount per serving | Calories 354 | Total Fat 13.7g | Saturated Fat 5.5g | Cholesterol 380mg | Sodium 1310mg | Total Carbohydrate 16.9g | Dietary Fiber 1.5g | Total Sugars 3.5g | Protein 40.2g

PREP
10 MIN

COOK
6 MIN

SERVES
4

Hearts of palm are delicious non-starchy vegetables that have a flavor reminiscent of artichokes. That's not their only feature, however—they also contain a whopping 17 different amino acids and fiber. You can find them canned or jarred at many grocery stores.

INGREDIENTS

- 2 small romaine hearts
- 1 cup hearts of palm, sliced
- 2 avocados, peeled, pitted, and chopped into cubes
- 2 tablespoons fresh lemon juice
- 1 tablespoon water
- 4 tablespoons extra virgin olive oil
- 1 teaspoon kosher salt, divided, or more to taste
- ½ teaspoon freshly ground black pepper, divided, or more to taste
- 1 tablespoon fresh chives, finely chopped
- 2 teaspoons fresh tarragon, finely chopped
- 1 ½ pounds raw scallops, dry packed
- 1 tablespoon avocado oil
- 4 lemon wedges, for serving

DIRECTIONS

Separate the lettuce leaves, rinse, and spin dry in a salad spinner. Arrange the lettuce leaves around the edges of four individual bowls. Top with equal amounts of hearts of palm and avocado.

In a small bowl, whisk together lemon juice, water, olive oil, half the salt and pepper, chives, and tarragon. Set aside.

Pat the scallops dry, removing any excess water, and season them with remaining salt and pepper.

Heat avocado oil in a skillet over medium-high heat. Once hot, sear the scallops for 3 minutes on one side and flip them over, searing for another 2 to 3 minutes.

Drizzle each salad with equal portions of dressing, reserving some for the scallops. Divide the cooked scallops between the bowls and drizzle over the remaining dressing. Serve immediately with fresh lemon wedges.

NUTRITION FACTS

Amount per serving | Calories 468 | Total Fat 33.4g | Saturated Fat 5.6g | Cholesterol 56mg | Sodium 1018mg | Total Carbohydrate 13.6g | Dietary Fiber 6.1g | Total Sugars 0.9g | Protein 31.3g

SPINACH AND SWEET POTATO CURRY
WITH BASMATI RICE

PREP
10 MIN

Indian white basmati rice is lower in lectins than other rice varieties but should be pressure cooked. Because it is still high in carbs, stick to half-cup servings. If you're early in your gut healing journey, I recommend avoiding all rice for at least a month. Cauliflower rice serves as a great gut-friendly substitute.

COOK
40 MIN

SERVES
6

INGREDIENTS

- 3 medium sweet potatoes, peeled and cut into large chunks
- 2 tablespoons extra virgin olive oil
- 5 cloves garlic, peeled and minced
- 1 teaspoon fresh ginger, peeled and minced
- 1 cup organic free-range chicken stock
- 1 cup low fat coconut milk
- ½ teaspoon cumin
- ½ teaspoon turmeric
- ½ teaspoon ground coriander
- ½ teaspoon black pepper
- 2 cups fresh spinach
- ½ cup cilantro, chopped
- 1 green onion, thinly sliced
- 1 ⅓ cups Indian White Basmati Rice, prepared according to package instructions

DIRECTIONS

Bring a large pot of water to a boil. Add the sweet potatoes and simmer for 7 to 10 minutes, until fork-tender. Drain and set aside.

Heat the oil in a large skillet over medium heat. Add garlic and ginger, and sauté for 2 minutes. Stir in the stock and coconut milk. Add cumin, turmeric, coriander, and black pepper. Stir and let simmer for 15 minutes.

Add in the drained sweet potatoes and cook for 10 minutes.

Cook the rice according to package instructions. Set aside.

Incorporate the spinach, cilantro, and green onion into the curry. Cook until the spinach is wilted and serve over the cooked rice.

NUTRITION FACTS
Amount per serving | Calories 321 | Total Fat 9.4g | Saturated Fat 4.7g | Cholesterol 0mg | Sodium 210mg | Total Carbohydrate 52.7g | Dietary Fiber 6.7g | Total Sugars 8.8g | Protein 8.4g

PREP
10 MIN

MARINATE
30 MIN

COOK
24 MIN

SERVES
6

White sweet potatoes are slightly lower in sugars and starch than their orange counterparts and are better able to pair with savory dishes. Here, they're combined with squid and fresh herbs for a totally new take on potato salad that is equally delicious served right away or as leftovers the next day.

INGREDIENTS

- 1 ½ pounds white sweet potato, cleaned, peeled, and cubed
- 2 pounds fresh squid, cleaned and sliced
- 2 teaspoons avocado oil
- ½ cup extra virgin olive oil
- 3 tablespoons fresh lemon juice
- 1 tablespoon parsley, finely chopped
- 2 teaspoons marjoram, chopped
- 1 clove garlic, grated
- ½ teaspoon kosher salt, or more to taste
- ½ teaspoon freshly ground black pepper, or more to taste

DIRECTIONS

Add potatoes to a large pot of salted water. Bring to a boil over high heat and cook for 15 to 20 minutes or until fork-tender. Drain sweet potatoes and set aside.

Add avocado oil to a medium frying pan and set over medium heat. Once hot, sauté the squid until tender and opaque 3 to 4 minutes.

In a large bowl, mix together the sweet potatoes, squid, and remaining ingredients and let sit for 30 minutes to marinate in the fridge before serving either cold or at room temperature.

NUTRITION FACTS

Amount per serving | Calories 386 | Total Fat 12.3g | Saturated Fat 2g | Cholesterol 352mg | Sodium 273mg | Total Carbohydrate 42.6g | Dietary Fiber 5.5g | Total Sugars 0.9g | Protein 25.8g

STIR-FRY CHICKEN WITH MUSHROOMS AND SWISS CHARD

Swiss chard is one of my favorite greens, especially the rainbow variety. I love the brightly colored red, magenta, orange, and yellow stems, which can be used like vegetables in almost any dish. If you want to use them in this dish, sauté them with the onions to soften their earthy taste.

PREP
15 MIN

COOK
15 MIN

SERVES
4

INGREDIENTS

- 2 tablespoons avocado oil
- 1 sweet onion, peeled and sliced
- 3 boneless, skinless, organic free-range chicken breasts, diced into bite-sized pieces (approx. 1 ¼ pounds total)
- 4 cloves garlic, peeled and minced
- 1 cup mushrooms, washed and sliced
- 1 tablespoon fresh lemon juice
- 5 tablespoons chicken stock
- 1 bunch Swiss chard, rinsed, trimmed, and chopped
- ½ teaspoon sea salt, or more to taste
- ½ teaspoon freshly ground black pepper, or more to taste
- 1 tablespoon extra virgin olive oil

DIRECTIONS

Add avocado oil to a large skillet or wok and set over medium heat. Sauté onion until soft and translucent, 5 to 7 minutes.

Add the chicken and continue to cook for 3 minutes, stirring occasionally. Add minced garlic and cook until fragrant, about 1 minute. Add the mushrooms, lemon juice, and chicken stock. Bring to a boil and cover the pan, cooking for an additional 3 to 5 minutes.

Add the Swiss chard and cook until wilted, about 2 minutes. Drizzle with olive oil and season to taste with sea salt and pepper.

Divide among plates and serve.

NUTRITION FACTS
Amount per serving | Calories 332 | Total Fat 15.1g | Saturated Fat 2.6g | Cholesterol 110mg | Sodium 425mg | Total Carbohydrate 5.1g | Dietary Fiber 1.2g | Total Sugars 1.8g | Protein 42.8g

PREP
5 MIN

COOK
15 MIN

While you won't find a carb-filled tortilla here, these "burritos" offer the same Mexican-inspired flavors as your favorite fast food burrito, with much healthier ingredients. To take it up a notch, add a healthy dollop of homemade guacamole for satisfying fat and gut-healing fiber.

SERVES
4

INGREDIENTS

— 2 medium sweet potatoes, scrubbed clean

— ½ cup cauliflower rice

— 1 teaspoon extra virgin olive oil

— ½ small lime, juiced

— ½ teaspoon kosher salt, divided, or more to taste

— 1 teaspoon avocado oil

— 1 small shallot, peeled and finely chopped

— 1 cup ground chicken

— ½ teaspoon ground cumin

— ½ teaspoon ground coriander

— ½ teaspoon dried oregano

— ¼ teaspoon freshly ground black pepper, or more to taste

— 1 cup fresh cilantro

— ½ small lime, cut into wedges, for serving

DIRECTIONS

With a fork, poke several small holes all over the sweet potatoes.

Place the sweet potatoes in microwave and cook for 6 to 8 minutes, until soft.

Cut the sweet potatoes in half and scoop out the insides, being sure to leave some sweet potato around the inside perimeter of the skin. Reserve the leftover sweet potato insides for a separate meal.

Add cauliflower rice to a small saucepan with the olive oil and sauté over medium-high heat for four minutes until tender. Add the lime juice and combine. Stir in ¼ teaspoon kosher salt and remove from the heat until ready to assemble.

In a medium sauté pan, heat the avocado oil over medium heat and sauté the shallot for 1 to 3 minutes or until softened. Add the ground chicken, cumin, coriander, oregano, remaining kosher salt and pepper. Continue to sauté until chicken is no longer pink and is thoroughly cooked, 5 to 10 minutes.

To assemble the "burritos," layer a large spoonful of cauliflower rice into each potato half. Top with the ground chicken mixture and garnish with cilantro leaves and lime wedges.

NUTRITION FACTS

Amount per serving | Calories 378 | Total Fat 10.3g | Saturated Fat 2.1g | Cholesterol 62mg | Sodium 666mg | Total Carbohydrate 49.1g | Dietary Fiber 8.1g | Total Sugars 2g | Protein 23.7g

SNACKS

Snacks are a fun and important part of the Healthy Gut Zone diet. They can boost your intake of fiber and polyphenols and will help keep you satisfied between meals. Make sure you get some protein with every meal or snack, while keeping vegetables the star of the plate. Remember: your gut bacteria thrive on the mix of vegetables, protein, and healthy additions like herbs, spices, and supportive fats. (Craving something sweet? Two squares of low-sugar dark chocolate per day—72 percent or higher—is a great source of polyphenols. I recommend eating it after dinner!)

SESAME SEED CRACKERS WITH SUNFLOWER AND PUMPKIN SEEDS AND ALMONDS

PREP
30 MIN

COOK
3 HR 30 MIN

SERVES
12

You don't need a fancy dehydrator to make perfectly crunchy gluten-free seed crackers—your oven is definitely up for the challenge. Filled with fiber and good fats that will be preserved thanks to the low cooking temperature, these crackers are a great alternative to expensive store-bought grain-free crackers and go well with every dip in this book.

INGREDIENTS

— 2 tablespoons avocado oil, plus more for greasing

— ¾ cup raw sesame seeds

— ¼ cup golden flax seeds

— ½ cup raw sunflower seeds

— 3 tablespoons raw pepitas

— 2 tablespoons raw almonds, chopped

— 2 tablespoons flax seeds

— 1 ½ teaspoons salt

DIRECTIONS

Preheat oven to 225°F. Line a standard-sized baking sheet with parchment paper and grease the paper with a drizzle of avocado oil.

In a large bowl, combine the sesame seeds, golden flax seeds, sunflower seeds, pepitas, almonds, and flax seeds with 1 ⅔ cups water. Stir and let stand while the seeds soften, about 20 minutes. Add salt and stir well to combine.

Spread the seed and nut mixture onto the tray in a thin, even layer. Brush the top with 2 tablespoons avocado oil before baking for 1 hour and 45 minutes.

Remove from the oven and carefully flip the cracker sheet over. Continue to bake the crackers until they are deep golden brown and crunchy, about 1 hour and 45 minutes longer. Let cool for 10 minutes before cutting out round crackers from the cracker sheet using a cookie cutter.

Transfer the crackers to cooling racks to cool completely before serving. Serve immediately, or store in an air-tight container.

NUTRITION FACTS
Amount per serving | Calories 131 | Total Fat 11.5g | Saturated Fat 1.5g | Cholesterol 0mg | Sodium 293mg | Total Carbohydrate 4.5g | Dietary Fiber 2.5g | Total Sugars 0.2g | Protein 3.8g

SPINACH AND KALE DIP

This gut-friendly take on spinach dip packs a heavy nutrient punch without the dairy or questionable oils of the traditional recipe. The creaminess comes from walnuts and avocado oil mayonnaise, making an indulgent dip for crackers and vegetables. It could also serve as a flavorful topping for fish or chicken.

PREP
15 MIN

COOK
15 MIN

SERVES
8

INGREDIENTS

— 4 tablespoons extra virgin olive oil, divided

— ⅓ cup raw walnut halves

— 2 cloves garlic, peeled and minced

— 3 cups baby spinach, washed, dried, and chopped

— 2 cups curly kale, thick stems removed, washed, and dried, leaves finely chopped

— ⅔ cup avocado oil mayonnaise

— 2 tablespoons fresh lemon juice

— ½ teaspoon salt

— ½ teaspoon freshly ground black pepper

— Assorted raw vegetables such as carrot sticks, broccoli florets, radishes, and celery, for serving

DIRECTIONS

In a large skillet, warm 2 tablespoons olive oil over medium heat. Add the walnuts and cook, stirring occasionally, until toasted and golden brown in spots, 6 to 8 minutes. Set aside to cool slightly, 5 to 10 minutes, then coarsely chop.

Heat the remaining 2 tablespoons olive oil in the same skillet over medium heat. Add the garlic and cook, stirring constantly until fragrant, about 1 minute.

Add the spinach and kale to the skillet and cook, stirring occasionally until just wilted, 3 to 5 minutes. Transfer the spinach and kale to a medium bowl and let cool slightly, about 10 minutes.

Once spinach and kale have cooled, add the mayonnaise, lemon juice, salt, pepper, and walnuts and stir to combine. Serve the dip immediately or store refrigerated in an air-tight container for up to 2 days. Serve with prepared raw vegetables.

NUTRITION FACTS
Amount per serving | Calories 183 | Total Fat 19.9g | Saturated Fat 2.7g | Cholesterol 20mg | Sodium 280mg | Total Carbohydrate 2.8g | Dietary Fiber 0.7g | Total Sugars 0.2g | Protein 1.2g

ASIAN-INSPIRED PICKLED GINGERED VEGETABLES

PREP
1 HR 20 MIN

REST
48 HR

SERVES
4

Pickles are one of my favorite snacks, and I like to think way beyond dilled cucumbers. Low in calories and high in fiber, this pickled vegetable mix—reminiscent of Korean kimchi—will satisfy your craving for something savory and salty with a nice crunch.

INGREDIENTS

- 1 small Napa cabbage, trimmed and shredded (approx. 4 cups)
- 1 small red cabbage, trimmed and shredded (approx. 2 cups)
- 1 tablespoon salt
- 3 cloves garlic, peeled and finely chopped
- 1 tablespoon fresh ginger, peeled and grated
- 3 tablespoons fish sauce
- 4 tablespoons rice wine vinegar
- ½ teaspoon freshly ground black pepper
- 2 medium carrots, peeled and julienned
- 2 scallions, sliced into ½-inch pieces
- 1 bunch small cilantro, leaves only, torn

DIRECTIONS

In a large bowl, combine the Napa cabbage and red cabbage with the salt. Toss well, cover, and set aside at room temperature until the cabbage has softened, about 1 hour.

Meanwhile, in a separate large bowl, whisk together the garlic, ginger, fish sauce, rice wine vinegar, and freshly ground black pepper.

Transfer the cabbage to a large fine-mesh strainer. Rinse with cold water and drain well. Add the cabbage to the bowl with the dressing along with the carrots, scallions, and cilantro. Toss the vegetables until well combined with the dressing. Transfer the vegetables to an air-tight container and refrigerate. They are good to eat after 2 days. Store the pickled vegetables refrigerated in the air-tight container for up to 2 weeks.

NUTRITION FACTS
Amount per serving | Calories 71 | Total Fat 0.4g | Saturated Fat 0.1g | Cholesterol 0mg | Sodium 2842mg | Total Carbohydrate 13.1g | Dietary Fiber 4.7g | Total Sugars 5.9g | Protein 3.3g

ROASTED SPICED CAULIFLOWER FLORETS

Popcorn is such a convenient and nostalgic snack, but most of the corn in America is GMO and high in carbs and lectins, therefore not advised for a gut-healthy lifestyle. This savory snack of roasted and spiced cauliflower florets offers that same big-bowl-of-flavor feeling without the gut guilt.

PREP
10 MIN

COOK
45 MIN

SERVES
4

INGREDIENTS

- 1 medium cauliflower, washed, cut into bite-sized florets
- 3 tablespoons extra virgin olive oil
- 1 teaspoon garlic powder
- 1 teaspoon ground cumin
- 1 teaspoon ground coriander
- 1 teaspoon salt
- 1 teaspoon freshly ground black pepper
- 1 tablespoon fresh flat-leaf parsley, finely chopped
- 1 lemon, cut into wedges

DIRECTIONS

Preheat oven to 425°F with racks in the upper and lower thirds of the oven. Line 2 baking sheets with parchment paper.

In a large bowl, combine the cauliflower, olive oil, garlic powder, cumin, coriander, salt, and pepper. Toss well to combine and spread out evenly on the two prepared baking sheets. Roast, tossing the cauliflower and rotating the pans once during the cooking process, until browned in parts and cooked through, 35 to 45 minutes.

Transfer the cauliflower to a serving bowl, sprinkle with parsley, and serve with lemon wedges. Serve immediately.

NUTRITION FACTS

Amount per serving | Calories 136 | Total Fat 10.8g | Saturated Fat 1.6g | Cholesterol 0mg | Sodium 627mg | Total Carbohydrate 10.1g | Dietary Fiber 4.3g | Total Sugars 4g | Protein 3.3g

CARROT DIP WITH ASSORTED VEGETABLES

PREP
15 MIN

COOK
15 MIN

SERVES
4

Spiced with flavorful cumin, ginger, and cinnamon, this carrot dip features Moroccan flavors and a beautiful bright orange color kids of all ages will love. In this recipe it's served with cauliflower, broccoli, celery, and radishes, but it would be equally delicious with cassava chips.

INGREDIENTS

- 1 pound carrots, washed, peeled, and thinly sliced
- 1 clove garlic, peeled
- ½ teaspoon ground cumin
- ½ teaspoon ground ginger
- ½ teaspoon ground cinnamon
- 1 teaspoon salt
- 2 tablespoons fresh lemon juice
- 3 tablespoons extra virgin olive oil, plus more for drizzling
- ½ small cauliflower, washed and cut into pieces
- ½ small broccoli, washed and cut into pieces
- 4 large celery stalks, washed and cut into pieces
- 4 large radishes, washed, trimmed, and cut into pieces

DIRECTIONS

Add a steamer basket to a medium saucepan and fill with 1 inch of water. Bring the water to a boil over high heat.

Once boiling, add the carrots and garlic clove, cover, and steam until the carrots and garlic are very tender, 4 to 6 minutes.

Transfer carrots and garlic to the bowl of a food processor and allow to cool for about 10 minutes before adding the cumin, ginger, cinnamon, salt, lemon juice, and olive oil. Process the carrot mixture until smooth.

Transfer the carrot dip to a serving bowl and drizzle with more olive oil. Serve the carrot dip along with prepared vegetables. Serve warm, room temperature, or cold.

NUTRITION FACTS

Amount per serving | Calories 200 | Total Fat 14.4g | Saturated Fat 2.1g | Cholesterol 0mg | Sodium 734mg | Total Carbohydrate 17.6g | Dietary Fiber 5.6g | Total Sugars 8g | Protein 2.9g

CAULIFLOWER FRITTERS WITH A CREAMY BASIL DIP

Cauliflower is the vegetable kingdom's chameleon. It can be used as a replacement for rice, pizza crust, popcorn (see p. 101), or even for potatoes in potato salad or mashed potatoes. In this recipe it stands on its own in a flavorful herbed fritter. If you're a fan of pesto, you'll also love this zesty, summery dip infused with fresh basil and lemon.

PREP
20 MIN

COOK
30 MIN
COOL
30 MIN

SERVES
4

INGREDIENTS

FRITTERS

- 1 large cauliflower, washed and cut into florets
- ½ cup coconut flour, plus ½ cup more for dusting
- 2 tablespoons flax seed meal
- 3 large eggs, lightly beaten
- 2 tablespoons fresh basil leaves, finely chopped
- ½ teaspoon salt
- ¼ teaspoon freshly ground black pepper
- 2 cups avocado oil

CREAMY BASIL DIP

- ⅓ cup avocado oil mayonnaise
- ⅓ cup fresh basil leaves, finely chopped
- 1 tablespoon fresh lemon zest
- 2 tablespoons fresh lemon juice
- ¼ teaspoon salt
- ¼ teaspoon freshly ground black pepper

DIRECTIONS

Add a steamer basket to a large saucepan and fill with 1 inch of water. Bring the water to a boil over high heat.

Once boiling, add the cauliflower florets, cover, and steam until the cauliflower is very tender, 6 to 8 minutes.

Transfer the cauliflower to the bowl of a food processor and let cool for about 10 minutes before pulsing until finely chopped. Transfer the cauliflower to a large bowl. Add ½ cup coconut flour, flax seed meal, eggs, basil, salt, and pepper and mix well to combine.

Use a small ice cream scoop or spoon to scoop out 2 to 3 tablespoons of the cauliflower batter. Using wet hands, gently shape the batter into a ball. Arrange the fritter on a baking sheet lined with parchment paper. Repeat this process with the remaining batter. Refrigerate until set, about 30 minutes.

Remove the fritters from the refrigerator. Place the remaining coconut flour in a bowl and lightly coat the fritters in the flour and return to the baking sheet.

In a medium saucepan, heat the oil over medium-high heat until it reaches 360°F. Working in batches, cook three or four fritters at a time until golden brown and crisp all over, turning once, about 2 to 3 minutes per side. Remove completed fritters to a paper towel-lined plate to drain.

In a small bowl, stir together the mayonnaise, basil, lemon zest, lemon juice, salt, and pepper until combined.

Transfer the fritters to a serving platter and serve immediately along with the dip.

NUTRITION FACTS

*Amount per serving | Calories 412 |
Total Fat 26.7g | Saturated Fat 6g |
Cholesterol 165mg | Sodium 700mg |
Total Carbohydrate 35.5g | Dietary Fiber 19.9g |
Total Sugars 5.8g | Protein 14.1g*

KALE CRISPS

PREP
10 MIN

COOK
35 MIN
COOL
30 MIN

SERVES
4

No matter how much you clean up your diet, the craving for crispy, crunchy chips will strike. When it does, it's kale crisps to the rescue! Make them simple with salt to start, then experiment with different flavorings like smoked paprika and cumin or sesame oil and ginger.

INGREDIENTS

— 1 pound curly kale, thick stems removed, washed, and dried well

— 2 tablespoons avocado oil

— 1 teaspoon kosher salt

DIRECTIONS

Preheat oven to 225°F, placing racks in the upper and lower thirds of the oven.

Tear the kale into 2-inch pieces. In a large bowl, toss the kale with the oil and salt and spread out between two large baking sheets.

Bake, rotating the trays and gently tossing the kale a couple times during cooking, until crisp and starting to turn golden, 25 to 35 minutes.

Remove the baking sheets from the oven to cooling racks, and cool completely before serving. Serve immediately or store at room temperature in an air-tight container for up to 3 days.

NUTRITION FACTS
Amount per serving | Calories 65 | Total Fat 0.9g | Saturated Fat 0.2g | Cholesterol 0mg | Sodium 631mg | Total Carbohydrate 12.2g | Dietary Fiber 2g | Total Sugars 0g | Protein 3.5g

PICKLED CARROTS

The following trio of pickled vegetables will add a rainbow of bright, crunchy snack options to your life. They're equally good on salads or in wraps as they are straight out of the jar. These carrots mimic the classic flavors of dill pickles, using both fresh dill and dill seeds.

PREP
10 MIN

COOK
20 MIN
CHILL
8 HR

SERVES
8

INGREDIENTS

- 1 pound carrots, washed, trimmed, peeled, and cut into 3- to 4-inch sticks
- 6 sprigs fresh dill
- 3 ¾ cups water
- 1 cup unfiltered apple cider vinegar
- 2 cloves garlic, peeled and lightly crushed
- 1 ½ tablespoons dill seeds
- 1 ½ tablespoons salt

DIRECTIONS

Fill a medium saucepan with 4 inches of water and bring to a boil over high heat. Have a large bowl of ice water ready.

Add carrots to the saucepan and cook until crisp tender, 2 to 3 minutes. Drain in a colander and transfer to the ice water bath to stop the cooking process. Drain the carrots again and divide the carrots and dill sprigs evenly between 2 quart-sized jars.

In a medium saucepan, combine the water, vinegar, garlic, dill seeds, and salt and bring to a boil over high heat. Turn off the heat and evenly divide the pickling liquid in the 2 jars of carrots. Let cool until room temperature, then cover and refrigerate 8 hours or up to 2 days before tasting. The carrots can be stored in the refrigerator for up to 1 month.

NUTRITION FACTS
Amount per serving | Calories 35 | Total Fat 0.2g | Saturated Fat 0g | Cholesterol 0mg | Sodium 478mg | Total Carbohydrate 8.6g | Dietary Fiber 1.7g | Total Sugars 2.8g | Protein 0.7g

PICKLED CAULIFLOWER

PREP
25 MIN

COOK
15 MIN
CHILL
8 HR

SERVES
12

In Southern Italy, pickled cauliflower is a classic example of giardiniera, or garden pickles. Cauliflower's firm texture really shines in a quick pickle, maintaining its crunch even after a week in the fridge. Here, the recipe gets a global makeover with cinnamon, cumin, ginger, and two kinds of peppercorns.

INGREDIENTS

- 1 medium cauliflower, washed, trimmed, cut into 2-inch florets
- ½ small, sweet onion, peeled and thinly sliced
- 5 garlic cloves, peeled and thinly sliced
- fresh ginger, 1-inch piece, peeled and sliced into ¼-inch-thick slices
- 1 cinnamon stick
- 1 teaspoon coriander seeds
- ½ teaspoon cumin seeds
- 2 cups unfiltered apple cider vinegar
- 2 tablespoons salt
- 1 teaspoon green peppercorns
- 1 teaspoon black peppercorns

DIRECTIONS

Add cauliflower, onion, garlic, and ginger either to a large bowl or to quart jars. Set aside.

In a medium saucepan, combine the cinnamon stick, coriander, and cumin seeds and toast over medium heat, stirring constantly until the spices are fragrant and slightly browned, 1 to 2 minutes.

Add vinegar, salt, peppercorns, and 1 cup water to the toasted spices and bring just to a boil over high heat. Turn off the heat and carefully pour the hot liquid over the vegetables.

Let cool to room temperature, then cover and refrigerate for at least 8 hours or up to 2 days before tasting. The veggies will keep for up to 2

weeks in the refrigerator.

NUTRITION FACTS

Amount per serving | Calories 27 | Total Fat 0.1g | Saturated Fat 0g | Cholesterol 0mg | Sodium 597mg | Total Carbohydrate 6.6g | Dietary Fiber 1.4g | Total Sugars 1.3g | Protein 1.2g

PICKLED FIDDLEHEADS

These curled fern fronds are picked off the tops of wild young ostrich ferns in the spring in the United States and Canada. They offer a healthy dose of potassium, iron, and even omega-3 fatty acids— plus an adorable and distinctive shape that just makes you want to smile. Can't find fiddlehead ferns? Asparagus or green beans are great substitutes.

PREP
10 MIN

COOK
20 MIN
CHILL
8 HR

SERVES
8

INGREDIENTS

— 2 pounds fiddlehead ferns, cleaned and ends trimmed

— 4 cloves garlic, peeled and crushed

— Peelings of 1 lemon

— 2 ½ tablespoons salt

— ½ teaspoon black peppercorns, lightly crushed

— 2 cups distilled white vinegar

NUTRITION FACTS
Amount per serving | Calories 44 |
Total Fat 0.5g | Saturated Fat 0g |
Cholesterol 0mg | Sodium 2184mg |
Total Carbohydrate 7.3g | Dietary Fiber 0.3g |
Total Sugars 0.3g | Protein 5g

DIRECTIONS

Fill a large saucepan with 3 inches of water and bring to a rolling boil over high heat. Have a large bowl of ice water ready.

Add the fiddleheads to the boiling water and cook until crisp tender, 4 to 5 minutes. Use a slotted spoon to transfer the fiddleheads to the bowl of ice water to stop the cooking process. Leave the fiddleheads in the water until very cold, about 10 minutes.

Drain the fiddleheads in a colander, then spread them out on dish cloths, pressing them with more cloths to extract as much liquid as possible.

Divide the fiddleheads between two quart-sized jars.

In a medium saucepan, combine the garlic, lemon peel, salt, and peppercorns with 4 cups water and bring to a boil over high heat. Remove from heat and stir in the vinegar. Pour the hot pickling liquid evenly into the two jars. Let cool to room temperature before covering the jars. Refrigerate for 8 hours or up to 2 days before tasting. The pickles can be stored in the refrigerator for up to 2 weeks.

PAN-FRIED MUSHROOMS
WITH THYME

PREP
10 MIN

COOK
10 MIN

SERVES
4

Wild mushrooms offer an array of gut-friendly benefits, from potent antioxidants to fiber and B vitamins. (They can be high in FODMAPs, so sensitive individuals should avoid eating them in large quantities.) Equally delicious as a snack or a savory side dish alongside eggs, chicken, or fish, these pan-fried wild mushrooms are both flavorful and elegant.

INGREDIENTS

- 2 tablespoons extra virgin olive oil
- 1 pound wild mushrooms, cleaned and sliced (approx. 6 cups)
- 2 cloves garlic, peeled and minced
- 3 fresh thyme sprigs, torn and divided
- 1 tablespoon unsweetened almond milk
- ½ teaspoon kosher salt, divided
- ½ teaspoon freshly ground black pepper

DIRECTIONS

Heat olive oil in a large skillet or cast iron pan set over medium heat. Add mushrooms and half the salt, sautéing until softened and starting to release their juices, about 4 to 5 minutes.

Stir in the garlic, half the thyme, and almond milk. Continue to sauté for a further 3 to 4 minutes until mushrooms are golden and very tender.

Remove from heat and season to taste with remaining salt and pepper. Garnish with remaining thyme just before serving.

NUTRITION FACTS
Amount per serving | Calories 98 | Total Fat 8.3g | Saturated Fat 1.9g | Cholesterol 0mg | Sodium 298mg | Total Carbohydrate 5.4g | Dietary Fiber 1.9g | Total Sugars 1.8g | Protein 3.4g

CREAMY AVOCADO AND HERB DIP

Love guacamole? Try this rich avocado dip for a fresh, herbaceous alternative. You can use any fresh herbs you have in addition to the ones below, including mint, cilantro, or dill. This dip also makes a great salad dressing or a base for a creamy chicken salad atop greens for an easy lunch.

PREP
15 MIN

COOK
15 MIN

SERVES
4

INGREDIENTS

- 2 medium ripe avocados

- 2 tablespoons extra virgin olive oil

- 2 tablespoons fresh lemon juice

- 1 clove garlic, peeled and minced

- ½ teaspoon salt

- ½ teaspoon freshly ground black pepper

- ½ cup fresh flat-leaf parsley, finely chopped

- ½ cup fresh basil leaves, chopped

- 2 tablespoons fresh chives, snipped

DIRECTIONS

Assorted raw vegetables—e.g., cauliflower florets, celery, and carrot sticks—for serving

Halve, pit, and peel the avocados. Transfer the flesh to a food processor, adding the olive oil, lemon juice, garlic, salt, pepper, and 3 tablespoons hot water.

Pulse to break down the avocado and then process on high until smooth and creamy, scraping down the sides as needed.

Transfer the avocado mixture to a medium bowl and gently stir in the parsley, basil, and chives. Serve immediately with prepared raw vegetables.

NUTRITION FACTS
Amount per serving | Calories 212 | Total Fat 20.5g | Saturated Fat 2.9g | Cholesterol 0mg | Sodium 304mg | Total Carbohydrate 8.7g | Dietary Fiber 6.3g | Total Sugars 0.5g | Protein 2.2g

CINNAMON AND COCOA ALMONDS

PREP
10 MIN

COOK
12 MIN

COOL
30 MIN

SERVES
4

This lightly sweet snack offers the health benefits of cocoa without the sugar and dairy of chocolate. Want a touch more sweetness? Add some monk fruit sugar or a pinch of stevia. If you don't have—or don't prefer—almonds, this recipe is equally delicious made with pecans or cashews.

INGREDIENTS

— 4 cups raw whole almonds, approx. 1 pound

— 2 tablespoons extra virgin olive oil

— 1 ¼ teaspoons ground cinnamon

— ½ teaspoon salt

— 3 tablespoons unsweetened cocoa powder

DIRECTIONS

Preheat oven to 350°F. Line a standard-sized baking sheet with parchment paper.

In a medium bowl, combine the almonds, olive oil, cinnamon, and salt and toss to combine. Spread the almonds out in a single layer on the prepared baking sheet.

Bake until evenly toasted, 9 to 12 minutes, flipping several times. Transfer the almonds to a large bowl to cool completely.

Place the cocoa powder in a fine mesh strainer and tap the strainer over the almonds while stirring them to coat in the cocoa powder. Serve immediately or store at room temperature in an air-tight container for up to 2 weeks.

NUTRITION FACTS

Amount per serving | Calories 310 | Total Fat 27.5g | Saturated Fat 2.5g | Cholesterol 0mg | Sodium 148mg | Total Carbohydrate 11.6g | Dietary Fiber 6.8g | Total Sugars 2.1g | Protein 10.5g

ROASTED THYME AND CUMIN SWEET POTATO ROUNDS

These roasted sweet potato "chips" are perfect for when you need a salty, savory snack. These pair well with any dip or spread, especially salsa and homemade guacamole for a delicious dose of good fat and fiber.

PREP
10 MIN

COOK
35 MIN

SERVES
4

INGREDIENTS

— 2 large sweet potatoes, scrubbed and sliced crosswise into ¼-inch thick rounds

— ¼ cup extra virgin olive oil

— 1 tablespoon fresh thyme leaves, finely chopped

— ¾ teaspoon ground cumin

— 1 teaspoon salt

— 1 teaspoon freshly ground black pepper

DIRECTIONS

Preheat oven to 425°F with racks in the upper and lower thirds of the oven. Line two standard-sized sheet pans with parchment paper.

In a large bowl, combine the potatoes, olive oil, thyme, cumin, salt, and pepper. Use hands or tongs to toss the sweet potatoes in the mixture until evenly coated.

Arrange the potato slices on the prepared sheet pans in a single layer, making sure not to overcrowd the pans.

Roast the sweet potatoes, flipping halfway through cooking, until tender and the edges are crisp and golden brown, 30 to 35 minutes. Serve immediately.

NUTRITION FACTS
Amount per serving | Calories 197 | Total Fat 7.4g | Saturated Fat 1.1g | Cholesterol 0mg | Sodium 593mg | Total Carbohydrate 32.3g | Dietary Fiber 5g | Total Sugars 0.6g | Protein 1.9g

A WEEK IN
THE HEALTHY GUT ZONE

DAY 1

BREAKFAST

- Organic coffee with 1 scoop MCT oil
- ½ to 1 teaspoon psyllium husk powder in 4 ounces of water
- Savory Cauliflower Breakfast Muffins (p. 22)
- ½ an avocado, sliced
- ¼ cup of berries

LUNCH

- Baked Ginger and Shallot Salmon and Bok Choy (p. 40)
- Asian-Inspired Pickled Gingered Vegetables (p. 100)

DINNER

- Lettuce Wrapped Veggie Burgers with Tangy Sauce (p. 82)
- Roasted Thyme and Cumin Sweet Potato Rounds (p. 111)

DAY 2

BREAKFAST

- Organic coffee with 1 scoop MCT oil
- ½ to 1 teaspoon psyllium husk powder in 4 ounces of water
- Sweet Potato "Toast" with Avocado and Smoked Salmon (p. 7)
- ¼ of cup berries

LUNCH

- 1 green banana
- Beef with Chinese Broccoli and Almonds (p. 41)

DINNER

- 1 small sweet potato (may add Pyure stevia and cinnamon)
- Roasted Chicken Legs with Green Mango Salsa (p. 86)

DAY 3

BREAKFAST

- Organic coffee with 1 scoop MCT oil
- ½ to 1 teaspoon psyllium husk powder in 4 ounces of water
- Chicken and Brussels Sprout Hash (p. 25)

LUNCH

- Mini Herb and Mushroom Frittatas (p. 50)
- Dandelion Salad with Pine Nuts in Lemon Dressing (p. 42)

DINNER

- Salmon Cakes with Cauliflower-Carrot Hash (p. 87)
- Broccoli and Spinach Soup (p. 76)

DAY 4

BREAKFAST

- Organic coffee with 1 scoop MCT oil
- ½ to 1 teaspoon psyllium husk powder in 4 ounces of water
- Breakfast Tacos on Cassava Tortillas (p. 13)
- ¼ cup of berries

LUNCH

- Shiitake Salmon Salad (p. 37)
- Pickled Fiddleheads (p. 107)

DINNER

- Seafood Soup with Curry Spices (p. 89)
- Roasted Spiced Cauliflower Florets (p. 101)

DAY 5

BREAKFAST

- Organic coffee with 1 scoop MCT oil
- ½ to 1 teaspoon psyllium husk powder in 4 ounces of water
- Savory Veggie Chiller (p. 11)
- Baked Eggs in Avocado (p. 12)

LUNCH

- Mini Chicken Burgers over Arugula Salad (p. 49)
- Roasted Sweet Potato Wedges with Ginger and Lime (p. 53)

DINNER

- Grilled Beef and Red Onion Kebabs (p. 80)
- Kale and Arugula Salad with Avocado and Walnuts (p. 36)

DAY 6

BREAKFAST

- Organic coffee with 1 scoop MCT oil
- ½ to 1 teaspoon psyllium husk powder in 4 ounces of water
- Green Shakshuka with Spinach and Pine Nuts (p. 19)
- Sweet Potato Hash (p. 20)

LUNCH

- Steamed Clams with Chimichurri and Lemon (p. 58)
- Roasted Asparagus with Citrus Vinaigrette (p. 52)

DINNER

- Carrot Dip with Assorted Vegetables (p. 102)
- Pan-Fried Trout Served with Roasted Brussels (p. 78)

DAY 7

BREAKFAST

- Organic coffee with 1 scoop MCT oil
- ½ to 1 teaspoon psyllium husk powder in 4 ounces of water
- Cassava Crepes with Coconut Yogurt and Mint-Cilantro Chutney (p. 16)
- ½ an avocado, sliced

LUNCH

- 1 green banana
- Salad Niçoise with Tuna, Egg, and Olives (p. 54)

DINNER

- Spinach and Sweet Potato Curry with Basmati Rice (p. 91)
- Green Asparagus Wrapped in Roast Beef (p. 79)